ADG-8638

YA
362.2955
MAR

SV

SANTA CRUZ CITY-COUNTY LIBRARY SYSTEM

I0575763

YOUNG ADULT 362.2955 MAR

Marijuana /

c2007.

6/08

SANTA CRUZ PUBLIC LIBRARY
SANTA CRUZ, CALIFORNIA 95060

INTRODUCING
ISSUES WITH
OPPOSING
VIEWPOINTS®

Marijuana

Other books in the Introducing Issues
with Opposing Viewpoints series:

Abortion
Advertising
AIDS
Alcohol
Animal Rights
Civil Liberties
Cloning
The Death Penalty
Drug Abuse
Drunk Driving
Energy Alternatives
The Environment
Euthanasia
Gangs
Gay Marriage
Genetic Engineering
Global Warming
Gun Control
Illegal Immigration
Islam
The Middle East
Military Draft
Obesity
Racism
Smoking
Teen Pregnancy
Terrorism
UFOs
Weapons of Mass Destruction

INTRODUCING
ISSUES WITH
OPPOSING
VIEWPOINTS®

Marijuana

Christine Van Tuyl, *Book Editor*

Christine Nasso, *Publisher*
Elizabeth Des Chenes, *Managing Editor*

GREENHAVEN PRESS
An imprint of Thomson Gale, a part of The Thomson Corporation

THOMSON
™
GALE

Detroit • New York • San Francisco • New Haven, Conn. • Waterville, Maine • London

© 2007 Thomson Gale, a part of The Thomson Corporation.

Thomson and Star Logo are trademarks and Gale and Greenhaven Press are registered trademarks used herein under license.

For more information, contact
Greenhaven Press
27500 Drake Rd.
Farmington Hills, MI 48331-3535
Or you can visit our Internet site at http://www.gale.com

ALL RIGHTS RESERVED.
No part of this work covered by the copyright hereon may be reproduced or used in any form or by any means—graphic, electronic, or mechanical, including photocopying, recording, taping, Web distribution or information storage retrieval systems—without the written permission of the publisher.

Articles in Greenhaven Press anthologies are often edited for length to meet page requirements. In addition, original titles of these works are changed to clearly present the main thesis and to explicitly indicate the author's opinion. Every effort is made to ensure that Greenhaven Press accurately reflects the original intent of the authors.

Every effort has been made to trace the owners of copyrighted material.

LIBRARY OF CONGRESS CATALOGING-IN-PUBLICATION DATA

Marijuana / Christine Van Tuyl, book editor.
    p. cm. — (Introducing issues with opposing viewpoints)
  Includes bibliographical references and index.
  ISBN-13: 978-0-7377-3574-1 (hardcover)
  1. Marijuana—United States. 2. Marijuana—Therapeutic use—United States. 3. Marijuana—Law and legislation—United States. 4. Drug legalization—United States. 5. Drug control—United States. I. Van Tuyl, Christine.
  HV5825.M343 2007
  362.29'55610973—dc22
                                                            2007003662

ISBN-10: 0-7377-3574-0
Printed in the United States of America

Contents

Foreword

I ndulging in a wide spectrum of ideas, beliefs, and perspectives is
a critical cornerstone of democracy. After all, it is often debates
over differences of opinion, such as whether to legalize abortion,
how to treat prisoners, or when to enact the death penalty, that shape
our society and drive it forward. Such diversity of thought is frequently regarded as the hallmark of a healthy and civilized culture. As the
Reverend Clifford Schutjer of the First Congregational Church in
Mansfield, Ohio, declared in a 2001 sermon, "Surrounding oneself
with only like-minded people, restricting what we listen to or read only
to what we find agreeable is irresponsible. Refusing to entertain doubts
once we make up our minds is a subtle but deadly form of arrogance."
With this advice in mind, Introducing Issues with Opposing Viewpoints
books aim to open readers' minds to the critically divergent views that
comprise our world's most important debates.

Introducing Issues with Opposing Viewpoints simplifies for students
the enormous and often overwhelming mass of material now available
via print and electronic media. Collected in every volume is an array of
opinions that captures the essence of a particular controversy or topic.
Introducing Issues with Opposing Viewpoints books embody the spir-
it of nineteenth-century journalist Charles A. Dana's axiom: "Fight for
your opinions, but do not believe that they contain the whole truth, or
the only truth." Absorbing such contrasting opinions teaches students
to analyze the strength of an argument and compare it to its opposi-
tion. From this process readers can inform and strengthen their own
opinions, or be exposed to new information that will change their minds.
Introducing Issues with Opposing Viewpoints is a mosaic of different
voices. The authors are statesmen, pundits, academics, journalists, cor-
porations, and ordinary people who have felt compelled to share their
experiences and ideas in a public forum. Their words have been collected from newspapers, journals, books, speeches, interviews, and the
Internet, the fastest growing body of opinionated material in the world.

Introducing Issues with Opposing Viewpoints shares many of the well-
known features of its critically acclaimed parent series, Opposing
Viewpoints. The articles are presented in a pro/con format, allowing readers to absorb divergent perspectives side by side. Active reading questions
preface each viewpoint, requiring the student to approach the material

thoughtfully and carefully. Useful charts, graphs, and cartoons supplement each article. A thorough introduction provides readers with crucial background on an issue. An annotated bibliography points the reader toward articles, books, and Web sites that contain additional information on the topic. An appendix of organizations to contact contains a wide variety of charities, nonprofit organizations, political groups, and private enterprises that each hold a position on the issue at hand. Finally, a comprehensive index allows readers to locate content quickly and efficiently.

Introducing Issues with Opposing Viewpoints is also significantly different from Opposing Viewpoints. As the series title implies, its presentation will help introduce students to the concept of opposing viewpoints, and learn to use this material to aid in critical writing and debate. The series' four-color, accessible format makes the books attractive and inviting to readers of all levels. In addition, each viewpoint has been carefully edited to maximize a reader's understanding of the content. Short but thorough viewpoints capture the essence of an argument. A substantial, thought-provoking essay question placed at the end of each viewpoint asks the student to further investigate the issues raised in the viewpoint, compare and contrast two authors' arguments, or consider how one might go about forming an opinion on the topic at hand. Each viewpoint contains sidebars that include at-a-glance information and handy statistics. A Facts About section located in the back of the book further supplies students with relevant facts and figures.

Following in the tradition of the Opposing Viewpoints series, Greenhaven Press continues to provide readers with invaluable exposure to the controversial issues that shape our world. As John Stuart Mill once wrote: "The only way in which a human being can make some approach to knowing the whole of a subject is by hearing what can be said about it by persons of every variety of opinion and studying all modes in which it can be looked at by every character of mind. No wise man ever acquired his wisdom in any mode but this." It is to this principle that Introducing Issues with Opposing Viewpoints books are dedicated.

Introduction

War on Marijuana

"What is it about . . . Cannabis, that causes such a diversity of opinion about it today?"

—Robert Deitch, *Hemp—American History Revisited: The Plant with a Divided History*

According to the United Nations Office on Drugs and Crime, "Cannabis continues to be, by far, the most widely used drug in the world." More than 100 million Americans aged twelve or older—or 40.2 percent of the population—have tried marijuana at least once in their lifetimes. More than 3.2 million Americans smoke it on a daily basis.

Yet, the fact remains that marijuana is illegal under federal law. The government has named marijuana a Schedule I drug, meaning that it is a dangerous, addictive substance with no known medical application. "The truth is, there are laws against marijuana because marijuana is harmful," argues John P. Walters, the director of the Office of National Drug Control Policy. So vehement is the government's stance on marijuana that many drug policy reform advocates claim that the war on drugs is really a war on marijuana.

The first law banning marijuana was passed in 1937, when lawmakers enacted the Marijuana Tax Act. The Bureau of Narcotics commissioner, Harry J. Anslinger, claimed that hemp plant should be banned because it had a violent "effect on the degenerate races," i.e., the Mexican immigrants entering the country for jobs during the Great Depression. Cannabis was blamed for causing murder, insanity, and death. The law passed quickly, but not without controversy. Despite its racist overtones, many commentators conclude that the law was passed just to prohibit industrial hemp from competing with paper, cotton, and newly discovered plastics like nylon.

The 1960s brought about the next major offensive against marijuana, while the counterculture movement fueled the drug's increasing popularity with singers and musicians touting the drug's many virtues. In response, Richard Nixon announced the commencement of the "War on Drugs," calling drugs "public enemy number one." The Nixon administration then passed the Controlled Substance Act of 1970 and established the Drug Enforcement Administration (DEA), a "super agency" that would handle all aspects of the drug problem. The Controlled Substance Act, which placed illicit and prescription substances into five categories, named marijuana a Schedule I drug, a category reserved for dangerous, addictive drugs.

Policy reform advocates attempted to get marijuana rescheduled several times and introduced bills in Congress, but none of their efforts were successful. In 1976 Jimmy Carter actually campaigned on the decriminalization of marijuana. Carter's head drug policy maker, Peter Bourne, publicly stated that he did not view marijuana—or even cocaine—as a serious public health threat.

"Just Say No" Campaign

Future policy makers disagreed. Dismayed by increased use of cocaine and crack in the early 1980s, then-First Lady Nancy Reagan launched her "Just Say No" antidrug campaign in 1984. Famous for the television ad, "This is your brain . . . this is your brain on drugs" as an egg sizzled in a skillet, and posters with the slogan, "Drugs Kill," the multimillion dollar campaign aimed to reduce youth drug use by aggressively infiltrating television, radio, and print media channels. Soon after, President Ronald Reagan signed a $1.7 billion drug bill along with requirements for mandatory sentencing of drug offenders. The Office of National Drug Control Policy (ONDCP) was also created to centrally coordinate legislative, security, diplomatic, research, and health policy throughout the government.

Although the "Just Say No" movement was in response to huge increases in cocaine and crack use among America's youth, the war on drugs quickly turned its attention to marijuana. Marijuana was quickly dubbed the "gateway drug" that led young people down the slippery slope of dangerous drug use and addiction.

Carlton Turner, Reagan's first director of the ONDCP, believed that marijuana use was inextricably linked to "the present young-adult generation's involvement in anti-military, anti-nuclear power, anti-big business, anti-authority demonstrations." At this time, a public-health approach to drug control was replaced by an emphasis on law enforcement. Drug abuse was no longer considered a form of illness, as all drug use was deemed immoral and deserving of staunch punishment. The drug war soon became a bipartisan effort, supported by liberals and conservatives alike.

Discovering Greater Dangers

Today, the drug office spends about $150 million a year on advertising, much of which funds antimarijuana campaigns. According to Ethan A. Nadelmann, the founder and executive director of the Drug Policy Alliance, law enforcement officers make about seven hundred thousand arrests each year for marijuana offenses. That is the same number of arrests for all other illicit drugs, including cocaine, heroin, and ecstasy, combined. According to recent studies, enforcing marijuana laws costs an estimated $10 to $15 million in direct costs alone. Roughly one hundred thousand Americans are behind bars for marijuana-related offenses, sparking intense debate about the rationale of demonizing a substance that has never caused a single death by overdose.

The U.S. government claims that strict policies are necessary because marijuana is so harmful. "With every year that passes, medical research discovers greater dangers from smoking it, from links to serious mental illness to the risk of cancer," according to Walters. He goes on to say that "marijuana does the most social harm of any illegal drug."

According to the Drug Enforcement Administration, marijuana is responsible for numerous health problems. Smoking marijuana leads to some changes in the brain that are similar to those caused by cocaine, heroin, and alcohol, asserts the DEA. In addition, regular marijuana users often develop breathing problems, including chronic coughing and wheezing. "Smoking five marijuana cigarettes is equal to smoking a full pack of tobacco cigarettes," claims the DEA.

According to the American Lung Association, there is 50 to 70 percent more cancer-causing material in marijuana smoke than in cigarette smoke. In addition, the number of marijuana-related emergency room visits has tripled in the last decade.

Just what is it about marijuana that makes it the subject of such heated controversy? Why does the U.S. government spend billions of dollars every year fighting it, and why do so many people seem to favor legalization, despite what the DEA tells us about its harms? These are some of the questions we hope to answer in this book, *Introducing Issues with Opposing Viewpoints: Marijuana.*

Chapter 1

Is Marijuana Harmful?

The effects of marijuana on the human body are frequently debated.

Marijuana Is Harmful to Your Health

National Center on Addiction and Substance Abuse at Columbia University (CASA)

"Smoking pot is a dangerous game of Russian roulette, not a harmless rite of passage."

Marijuana is a dangerous drug, asserts the National Center on Addiction and Substance Abuse at Columbia University (CASA). Research proves that marijuana harms the brain, the lungs, the heart, and the reproductive system. Marijuana-related emergency room admissions have been on the rise since the late 1990s, making it the second most frequently mentioned drug in emergency room admissions. Educating the public about the dangers of marijuana use is paramount to CASA, a national organization that combats the abuse of all substances.

AS YOU READ, CONSIDER THE FOLLOWING QUESTIONS:
1. To what does CASA attribute the significant increase in the number of marijuana-related emergency room admissions?
2. According to CASA, what sorts of respiratory problems do marijuana smokers exhibit?
3. According to the Substance Abuse and Mental Health Services Administration, how does marijuana affect the reproductive system?

The National Center on Addiction and Substance Abuse at Columbia University (CASA), Non-Medical Marijuana II: Rite of Passage or Russian Roulette?, New York, NY: The National Center on Addiction and Substance Abuse at Columbia University (CASA), 2004. Copyright © 2004. All rights reserved. Reproduced by permission.

Research on the risks and dangers of using marijuana is ongoing, and we do not yet fully understand all of the implications of using marijuana and its effects on organ systems and behavior. But the more researchers study the drug and the consequences of its use, the clearer it becomes that smoking pot is a dangerous game of Russian roulette, not a harmless rite of passage.

Marijuana-Related Medical Emergencies on the Rise

Marijuana-related medical emergencies are on the rise among young people. According to the Drug Abuse Warning Network Survey (DAWN), emergency department mentions of marijuana increased 37.2 percent between 1999 and 2002, from 87,068 to 119,472. The increase among 12- to 17-year-olds was 48 percent.

Patients age 6 to 25 accounted for half (47 percent) of the emergency department mentions of marijuana in 2002. Marijuana was the second most frequently mentioned illicit substance in emergency rooms in 2002 (accounting for 18 percent of mentions), following cocaine (30 percent of mentions). The third most frequently mentioned illicit substance in 2002 was heroin.

FAST FACT

The British Lung Foundation reports that smoking three or four marijuana joints is as bad for your lungs as smoking twenty cigarettes.

Marijuana may be the only drug mentioned or one of five drugs mentioned. What is of concern is the comparative data—the significant increase in the number of mentions over a three-year period and the likelihood that this increase is related to the increased potency of the drug. . . .

Marijuana and the Brain

Recent research findings indicate that long-term use of marijuana produces changes in the brain similar to those seen after long-term use of other drugs of abuse, such as cocaine and opiates. THC, the main psychoactive or mind-altering ingredient in marijuana, binds to and activates receptors in the brain called cannabinoid receptors,

Marijuana's Effects on the Brain

Brain regions in which cannabinoid receptors are abundant

Brain Region	Functions Associated with Region
Cerebellum	Body movement coordination
Hippocampus	Learning and memory
Cerebral cortex, especially cingulate, frontal, and parietal regions	Higher cognitive functions
Nucleus accumbens	Reward

Basal ganglia
  Substantia nigra pars reticulata
  Entopeduncular nucleus
  Globus pallidus
  Putamen
	Movement control

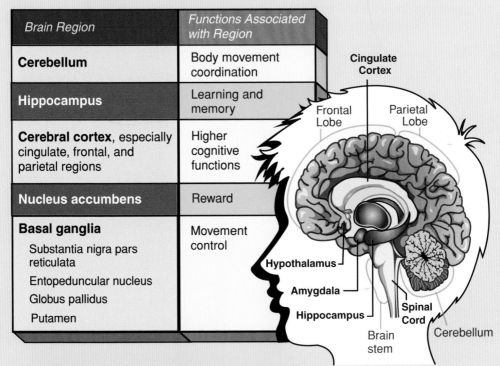

Brain regions in which cannabinoid receptors are moderately concentrated

Brain Region	Functions Associated with Region
Hypothalamus	Body housekeeping functions (body temperature regulation, salt and water balance, reproductive function)
Amygdala	Emotional response, fear
Spinal cord	Peripheral sensation, including pain
Brain stem	Sleep and arousal, temperature regulation, motor control
Central gray	Analgesia
Nucleus of the solitary tract	Visceral sensation, nausea and vomiting

Source: Reprinted from the National Institute on Drug Abuse.

changing the way sensory information gets into the brain and is processed there. There are cannabinoid receptors in different regions of the brain, including the cerebellum (responsible for balance and coordination of movement) and the hippocampus (crucial for learning and memory). THC affects memory by activating cannabinoid receptors in the hippocampus and decreasing the activity of neurons in this area of the brain.

Long-term marijuana use causes temporary cognitive defects, particularly with respect to attention and memory, lasting as long as a few days after smoking marijuana. The cognitive impairments that marijuana causes have been found to worsen with increasing years of use. Even short-term losses of cognitive functions as a result of marijuana use are detrimental, especially to the developing minds of children and adolescents. A study of college students reveals that critical skills related to attention, memory and learning are impaired among those who use marijuana heavily (an average of 29 out of 30 days), even after discontinuing its use for at least 24 hours. The U.S. Department of Education notes that the use of marijuana is detrimental to young people not only because the drug affects the ability to concentrate and, therefore, master important academic skills, but also because "teens who rely on marijuana as a chemical crutch and refuse to face the challenges of growing up never learn the emotional, psychological, and social lessons of adolescence." Researchers have found a relationship between marijuana and schizophrenia, psychosis and depression; further work is necessary to determine whether marijuana triggers the onset of schizophrenia or depression in otherwise vulnerable people, whether it causes these conditions in non-predisposed people, or whether it does both.

Marijuana and the Lungs

Regular marijuana smokers display many of the respiratory problems of tobacco smokers, including daily cough and phlegm, symptoms of chronic bronchitis, more frequent chest colds and damage to lung tissue. Habitual use of marijuana is associated with frequent respiratory symptoms, including chronic bronchitis, acute bronchitis and wheezing.

Regardless of the THC content, the amount of tar inhaled by marijuana smokers and the level of carbon monoxide absorbed are three to five times greater than among tobacco smokers. This may be due to marijuana users inhaling more deeply and holding the smoke in their lungs. Another recent finding is that marijuana use can interfere with tobacco cessation attempts: one study found that tobacco smokers who also smoke marijuana may be less likely to quit smoking tobacco—and even less likely to try to quit—than those who do not smoke marijuana.

Marijuana and the Heart

Marijuana use causes a 20 percent to 100 percent increase in heart rate, starting during the ten minutes or so it takes to smoke a marijuana cigarette and lasting two to three hours, as well as increases in cardiac output (the volume of blood pumped by the heart per minute). Cardiac function is altered for some hours after marijuana use.

Within the first hour of smoking, marijuana users have been found to be five times likelier to have a heart attack than non–marijuana smokers; within the second hour, the risk declines to 1.7 times normal and returns to an average risk after two hours.

Scientists believe smoking marijuana puts a strain on your heart but are not sure whether it is the active ingredient THC itself or other substances within the inhaled smoke, such as carbon monoxide and burnt plant particles, that have such negative effects. Further research is necessary to understand the relationship of marijuana use to cardiovascular disease.

Marijuana, Fertility, and Pregnancy

Chronic marijuana use has been shown to shorten women's menstrual cycles and can impact the female reproductive system by elevating prolactin hormone levels and depressing testosterone levels. Men who smoke marijuana about four times a week have been found to have reduced volumes of semen and sperm, and to have sperm that move at abnormally high velocity; such sperm may burn out quickly and reduce fertility in men.

Women who smoke marijuana during pregnancy often have children with low birth weights, and researchers have observed that "there is evidence that infants exposed in utero to cannabis [may] have behavioral and developmental effects during the first few months after birth.

Members of Students Against Destructive Decisions rally in Houston in 2002, urging commuters to talk to their kids about the harmful effects of using marijuana.

Between the ages of four and nine years, exposed children have showed deficits in sustained attention, memory and higher cognitive functioning."...

More Dangers

We know more today than we ever have about the dangers of marijuana use to America's teens and children. The drug is more potent than it was in the past, there is more data on the short- and long-term health impacts of using marijuana, and more emergency room mentions and treatment admissions are associated with the use of marijuana. The evidence continues to mount for a connection between the use of marijuana and the later use of other illegal drugs.

Most people who smoke pot do not move on to other drugs, but then only five to seven percent of cigarette smokers get lung cancer. The point is that those youngsters who smoke pot are at vastly greater risk of moving on to other drugs. The potential of marijuana as a dangerous drug in and of itself, and as a gateway to other drug use, is a matter of serious concern for American parents, especially in light of the drug's pervasive presence in their teenagers' lives.

Nonetheless, many teens and their parents view marijuana use as a harmless recreation. This perception is inaccurate and dangerous, because perceptions and attitudes among teens and their parents are a key factor in teens' decisions about using drugs. It is imperative that teens, parents, teachers, communities and policymakers be made aware of the most current information about marijuana use and its consequences. Research on the risks and dangers of using marijuana is ongoing, and we do not yet fully understand all of the implications of using marijuana and its effects on organ systems and behavior. But the more researchers study the drug and the effects of its use, the clearer it becomes that smoking pot is a dangerous game of Russian roulette, not a harmless rite of passage.

EVALUATING THE AUTHORS' ARGUMENTS:

In the viewpoint you just read CASA argues that marijuana is a dangerous substance that is responsible for several health problems. Is CASA's argument convincing? Would these arguments be effective in arguing that marijuana should not be legalized?

Marijuana Is Rarely Harmful to Your Health

"Almost all drugs— including those that are legal— pose greater threats to individual health and/ or society than does marijuana."

Paul Armentano

Policy makers, law enforcement, and the U.S. government grossly exaggerate marijuana's potential harms, according to Paul Armentano, chairman and president of NORML, the National Organization for the Reform of Marijuana Laws. The truth is, most other drugs—including legal prescription drugs—are far more harmful than marijuana. Marijuana is not a causal factor in emergency room admissions, nor does it harm the brain as do other drugs like cocaine. According to Armentano, marijuana's risk to the individual and society do not warrant criminal prohibition and the arrest of 750,000 Americans every year.

AS YOU READ, CONSIDER THE FOLLOWING QUESTIONS:
1. According to Armentano, what are the ramifications of exaggerating marijuana's harms?
2. What facts does the author use to support the argument that tobacco and alcohol are more harmful than marijuana?

Armentano, Paul. The 2005 NORML Truth Report, Washington, DC: NORML Foundation, 2005. Copyright © 2005 NORML. Reproduced by permission.

3. To what does the author attribute the rise in marijuana admissions to drug rehabilitation clinics?

NORML believes there is nothing to be gained by exaggerating claims of marijuana's harms. On the contrary, by overstating marijuana's potential risk, America's policy-makers and law enforcement community undermine their credibility and ability to effectively educate the public of the legitimate harms associated with more dangerous drugs. In addition, exaggerating the dangers associated with the responsible use of marijuana results in the needless arrest of hundreds of thousands of good, productive citizens each year in this country. . . .

Let's allow science, not rhetoric, to dictate America's public policy regarding marijuana. As you will see, the facts speak for themselves. . . .

Marijuana's Harms Are Overstated

The statement [that "Nationwide, no drug matches the threat posed by marijuana"] is pure hyperbole. *By overstating marijuana's potential harms, America's policy-makers and law enforcement community undermine their credibility and ability to effectively educate the public of the legitimate harms associated with more dangerous drugs like heroin, crack cocaine, and methamphetamine.*

In fact, almost all drugs—including those that are legal—pose greater threats to individual health and/or society than does marijuana. According to the Centers for Disease Control, approximately 46,000 people die each year from alcohol-induced deaths (not including motor vehicle fatalities where alcohol impairment was a contributing factor), such as overdose and cirrhosis. Similarly, more than 440,000 premature deaths annually are attributed to tobacco smoking. By comparison, marijuana is non-toxic and cannot cause death by overdose. In a large-scale population study of marijuana use and mortality published in the *American Journal of Public Health*, marijuana use, even long-term, "showed little if any effect . . . on non-AIDS mortality in men and on total mortality in women."

After an exhaustive, federally commissioned study by the National Academy of Sciences' Institute of Medicine (IOM) in 1999 examining all of marijuana's potential health risks, authors concluded, "*Except for the harms associated with smoking, the adverse effects of marijuana use are within the range tolerated for other medications.*" (It should be noted that many risks associated with marijuana and smoking may be mitigated by alternative routes of administration such as vaporization.) The IOM further added, "*There is no conclusive evidence that marijuana causes cancer in humans, including cancers usually related to tobacco use.*" A 2001 large-scale case-controlled study affirmed this finding, concluding that "the balance of evidence . . . does not favor the idea that marijuana as commonly used in the community is a major causal factor for head, neck, or lung cancer." More recently, a 2004 study published in the journal *Cancer Research* con-

FAST FACT

There has never been a single documented overdose from consuming marijuana.

cluded that cannabis use is not associated with an increased risk of developing oral cancer "regardless of how long, how much, or how often a person has used marijuana."

Numerous studies and federally commissioned reports have endorsed marijuana's relative safety compared to other drugs, and recommended its decriminalization or legalization. Virtually all of these studies have concluded that the criminal "*classification of cannabis is disproportionate in relation both to its inherent harmfulness, and to the harmfulness of other substances.*" Even a pair of editorials by the premiere British medical journal, *The Lancet*, acknowledge: "The smoking of cannabis, even long-term, is not harmful to health. . . . It would be reasonable to judge cannabis as less of a threat . . . than alcohol or tobacco." Indeed, *by far the greatest danger to health posed by the use of marijuana stems from a criminal arrest and/or conviction.*

Claims of Marijuana Addiction Are Grossly Exaggerated
[Some government organizations claim that] 60 percent of teenagers in treatment have a primary marijuana diagnosis. This means that the addiction to marijuana by our youth exceeds their

addiction rates for alcohol, cocaine, heroin, methamphetamine, ecstasy and all other drugs combined.

This statement is purposefully misleading. Although admissions to drug rehabilitation clinics among marijuana users have increased dramatically since the mid-1990s, *this rise in marijuana admissions is due to a proportional increase in the number of people arrested by law enforcement for marijuana violations and subsequently referred to drug treatment by the criminal justice system.* **Primarily, these are young people arrested for minor possession offenses, brought before a criminal judge (or drug court), and ordered to rehabilitation in lieu of jail or juvenile detention**. As such, this data is in no way indicative of whether the person referred to treatment is suffering from any symptoms of dependence associated with marijuana use; most individuals are ordered to attend supervised drug treatment simply to avoid jail time. In fact, *since 1995, the proportion of admissions from*

U.S. National Drug Control Policy director John Walters (l) and U.S. attorney McGregor Scott pull out marijuana plants while touring a pot garden busted by authorities in California in 2006.

all sources other than the criminal justice system has actually declined, according to the federal Drug and Alcohol Services Information System (DASIS). Consequently, DASIS now reports that 58 percent of all marijuana admissions are through the criminal justice system. Referrals from schools and health care/drug abuse care providers comprise another 15 percent of all admissions. By comparison, only 38 percent of those admitted to treatment for alcohol and only 29 percent of those admitted to treatment for cocaine are referred by the criminal justice system. . . .

Marijuana's Risk to Society Is Minor

The statement [that "marijuana is not harmless"] is correct; marijuana isn't harmless. In fact, no substance is, including those that are legal. However, any risk presented by marijuana smoking falls within the ambit of choice we permit the individual in a free society. According to federal statistics, approximately 80 million Americans self-identify as having used marijuana at some point in their lives, and relatively few acknowledge having suffered significant deleterious health effects due to their use. America's public policies should reflect this reality, not deny it.

Marijuana's relative risk to the user and society does not support criminal prohibition or the continued arrest of more than 750,000 Americans on marijuana charges every year. As concluded by the Canadian House of Commons in their December 2002 report recommending marijuana decriminalization, *"The consequences of conviction for possession of a small amount of cannabis for personal use are disproportionate to the potential harm associated with the behavior."*

Marijuana-Related Emergency Room Admissions Are Overstated

The statement [that "as a factor in emergency room visits, marijuana has risen 176 percent since 1994, and now surpasses heroin"] is intentionally misleading as it wrongly suggests that marijuana use is a significant causal factor in an alarming number of emergency room visits. It is not.

Federal statistics gathered by the Drug Abuse Warning Network (DAWN) do indicate an increase in the number of people "mentioning"

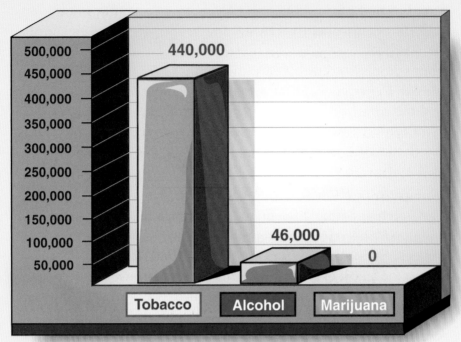

Annual Deaths

- 500,000
- 450,000
- 400,000
- 350,000
- 300,000
- 250,000
- 200,000
- 150,000
- 100,000
- 50,000

440,000 — Tobacco
46,000 — Alcohol
0 — Marijuana

Source: Centers for Disease Control.

marijuana during hospital emergency room visits. (This increase is hardly unique to marijuana however, as the overall number of drug mentions has risen dramatically since the late 1980s—likely due to improved federal reporting procedures.) However, **a marijuana "mention" does not mean that marijuana caused the hospital visit** or that it was a factor in leading to the ER episode, only that the patient said that he or she had used marijuana previously.

For every emergency room visit related to drug use (so-called "drug abuse episodes"), hospital staff list up to five drugs the patient reports having used recently, regardless of whether or not their use of the drug caused the visit. The frequency with which any drug is mentioned in such visits is generally proportional to its frequency of use, irrespective of its inherent dangers. . . .

Marijuana Does Not Harm the Brain

Allegations that marijuana smoking alters brain function or has long-term effects on cognition are reckless and scientifically unfounded.

Federally sponsored population studies conducted in Jamaica, Greece and Costa Rica found no significant differences in brain function between long-term smokers and non-users. Similarly, a 1999 study of 1,300 volunteers published in *The American Journal of Epidemiology* reported "*no significant differences in cognitive decline between heavy users, light users, and nonusers of cannabis*" over a 15-year period. Most recently, a meta-analysis of neuropsychological studies of long-term marijuana smokers by the National Institute on Drug Abuse reaffirmed this conclusion. In addition, a study published in the *Canadian Medical Association Journal* in April [2005] reported that even former heavy marijuana smokers experience no negative measurable effects on intelligence quotient.

Claims specifically charging that marijuana leads to brain changes similar to those induced by heroin and cocaine are based solely on the results of a handful of animal studies that demonstrated that THC (delta-9-tetrahydrocannabinol, the main psychoactive ingredient in marijuana) can stimulate dopamine production under certain extreme conditions, and that the immediate cessation of THC (via the administration of a chemical blocking agent) will initiate some mild symptoms of withdrawal. These findings have little bearing on the human population because, according to the US Institute of Medicine, "The long half-life and slow elimination from the body of THC . . . prevent[s] substantial abstinence symptoms" in humans. As a result, such symptoms have only been identified in rare, unique patient settings—limited to adolescents in treatment for substance abuse, or in clinical research trials where volunteers are administered marijuana or THC daily.

EVALUATING THE AUTHOR'S ARGUMENTS:

In the viewpoint you just read Armentano refutes some of the main points made in the previous viewpoint, "Marijuana Is Harmful to Your Health." Did he do a convincing job of refuting all the arguments? What did he fail to address?

Viewpoint

3

Marijuana Adversely Affects Safe Driving Skills

Jim Porter

"Marijuana intoxication can . . . seriously affect driving skills."

Marijuana has detrimental effects on the skills needed for safe driving and plays a major role in traffic accidents, asserts Jim Porter in his article "Marijuana and Driving: Going to Pot on the Highway." Tests have shown that marijuana can distort perceptions, impair judgment, and severely diminish complex motor tasks critical to safe driving. Other effects include a drop in roadside alertness, concentration, motor coordination, and the ability to react quickly to emergency situations. Compounding the problem, most of the subjects noted in past studies were tested with marijuana that is two to fifteen times less potent than what people are actually smoking today. According to the article, published on the Friendsdrivesober.org Web site, it is inadvisable to operate any vehicle or dangerous equipment under the influence of marijuana.

Porter, Jim. "Marijuana and Driving: Going to Pot on the Highway," Friendsdrivesober.org, October, 2003. Copyright © 2004 Friends Drive Sober.org. Reproduced by permission of the author.

AS YOU READ, CONSIDER THE FOLLOWING QUESTIONS:
  1. According to this viewpoint, how does marijuana affect safe driving skills?
  2. According to Porter, how many traffic accidents is marijuana responsible for?
  3. How are THC levels changing in marijuana?

D riving is probably the most complex psychomotor task undertaken by everyday people on a routine basis. Many people actually believe that they operate a motor vehicle safely and efficiently when driving under the influence of marijuana. A number of new studies have been conducted to determine marijuana's effect on driving performance using state-of-the-art driving simulators, laboratory investigations and highway courses, both closed and open.

Effects on Driving

A current literature search that includes outcomes from valid medical marijuana studies reveals that marijuana can damage short term memory, distort perceptions, and impair judgment and complex motor skills while altering heart rate. Marijuana intoxication can also cause anxiety attacks, paranoia and lethargy, which can seriously affect driving skills. . .

The Institute of Medicine's (IOM) medical marijuana study team contends in their federally published report that "For most people, the primary adverse effect of acute marijuana use is diminished psychomotor performance. It is, therefore, inadvisable to operate any vehicle or potentially dangerous equipment while under the influence of marijuana, THC or any cannabinoid drug with comparable effects."

Other Studies

In research using a driving simulator, marijuana use before driving has seriously impacted the skills necessary to operate a vehicle safely. Roadside alertness is severely diminished as is concentration, motor coordination and the ability to react quickly. Research subjects found it difficult to judge distance and react appropriately to roadside signals and sounds after smoking marijuana. These effects were still present in the research subjects 24 hours later, demonstrating that the impairment continued long after the "high" was gone.

In a laboratory study at the National Institute on Drug Abuse (NIDA) Addiction Research Center, study subjects were asked to smoke a marijuana cigarette, wait 10 minutes, and then smoke another cigarette. Both cigarettes contained either 0, 1.8, or 3.6 percent THC-Δ9, the main psychoactive compound in cannabis. Twenty minutes after smoking the cigarettes, the subjects were given a standard roadside sobriety test similar to those used to test drivers suspected of using alcohol. The outcomes showed that marijuana significantly impaired their ability to stand on one leg for 30 seconds or touch their finger to their nose. As the dose of THC increased, the subjects swayed

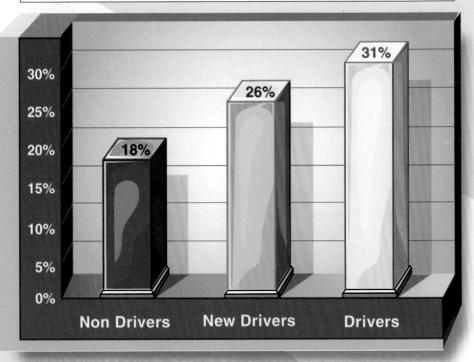

Percentage of Students Who Used Marijuana (High school students surveyed in spring 2002)

Source: *Journal of Studies on Alcohol* (vol. 65, pp. 289–96), May 2004.

more, raised their arms or put their feet down in an attempt to maintain their balance. Subjects also committed 2.5 times more errors when they attempted to touch their finger to their nose.

Higher THC Levels

This writer takes note that in all of the driver simulator studies and closed course research that I have reviewed over the last decade, test subjects are given marijuana cigarettes that have between 1.5 to 4 percent tetrahydrocannabinol, Delta 9 (THC-Δ9). THC-Δ9 is the main psychoactive compound found in *Cannabis sativa, Cannabis indica* and related hybrid plants that are cultivated for their intoxicating properties. In my investigative inquiries with police forces, drug testing labs and chronic marijuana users that I meet in treatment, I am told that the marijuana of today (Kind Bud, CBC, Neiterwiet, Skunk Weed, White Widow, etc.) is testing out at 8 to 35 percent THC-Δ9. The reality of these findings mean that test subjects in these current studies are demonstrating impairment with marijuana that is 2 to 15 times less potentiated than what people are actually consuming in today's illicit-drug marketplace.

FAST FACT

In 2002 almost 11 million people drove under the influence of illegal drugs.

Major Role in Traffic Accidents

Contrary to popular belief, marijuana has been found to play a significant role in car accidents across the United States with as much as 33 percent of drivers arrested at the scene of the accident being positive for marijuana and another 12 percent testing positive for both marijuana and cocaine. Every year, 28 percent of all drivers in the United States will attempt to drive within two hours after ingesting alcohol or illicit drugs. Marijuana is the illicit drug used most often (70%) by drivers who drove after drug use and is a major factor why motor vehicle crashes are the leading cause of death for American young people.

A member of the group Cannabis Action London makes a marijuana joint. In 2002 the British government announced its intention to downgrade marijuana from a Class B drug to a Class C drug, making possession and use a less serious offense.

In an intergovernmental contact between the United States National Highway Traffic Safety Administration (NHTSA) and the Dutch Ministry of Transport, two studies were conducted on real roads in normal traffic to objectively measure both marijuana and alcohol effects, separate and combined, on actual driving performance. The test vehicles were outfitted with redundant driving controls that were managed by a licensed driving instructor who monitored and rated the subjects' driving abilities. The investigators concluded that the effects of THC alone on driving performance were of sufficient magnitude to warrant concern due to the subjects' level of impairment and inability to facilitate evasive action if necessary. The investigators also reported that THC impaired drivers were more likely to fall asleep during prolonged vehicle operation. Both studies found that marijuana and low doses of alcohol (.04 BAC [blood alcohol content], less than two drinks in an hour) interact additively to produce greater impairment for drivers than the sum of changes that each drug produces separately. Both studies concluded that THC and alcohol use in combination creates a serious threat to highway safety as many of the test subjects would have been involved in collisions were it not for the interventions of the driving instructor that was monitoring them.

EVALUATING THE AUTHOR'S ARGUMENTS:

In the viewpoint you just read Porter argues that marijuana is a major factor in traffic accidents. Are his arguments compelling? Why or why not?

Marijuana Does Not Affect Safe Driving Skills

Dale Gieringer

> *"Drivers with lower levels of marijuana have been found to be no more dangerous . . . than other drivers."*

Marijuana does not pose a major threat to highway safety, according to Dale Gieringer, coordinator of California NORML. Recent studies have shown that drivers with low levels of marijuana are no more dangerous, and often even safer, than other drivers. In fact, one study showed that marijuana produces greater caution in drivers, because the users are aware of their state and compensate for it. Alcohol is a much greater hazard to highway safety, as it encourages speeding and risky behavior. In his report *Driving Studies Show Limited Accident Risk from Marijuana* Gieringer argues that there is no evidence that marijuana has contributed significantly to highway accidents.

AS YOU READ, CONSIDER THE FOLLOWING QUESTIONS:

1. The author argues that marijuana does not affect safe driving skills. What studies does he use to support this?
2. According to the author, what substance is much more dangerous to safe driving skills than marijuana?

California NORML Research Report, May, 2005. Copyright © 2005 California NORML. Reproduced by permission.

3. According to the viewpoint, how does marijuana encourage greater caution in drivers?

Scientific studies on marijuana and driving fail to support the notion that marijuana poses a significant public highway safety hazard, according to evidence compiled by NORML [National Organization for the Reform of Marijuana Laws].

In particular, the evidence fails to support proposals by marijuana opponents to impose tough new "zero-tolerance" standards for driving under the influence of marijuana or to disallow on-site use in medical cannabis clubs out of fear for driving safety.

In general, the evidence shows that marijuana is a lesser traffic hazard than alcohol or other drugs. Marijuana appears to be most dangerous in high doses, or when combined with alcohol. On the other hand, drivers with lower levels of marijuana have been found to be no more dangerous, and in some cases arguably safer, than other drivers. . . .

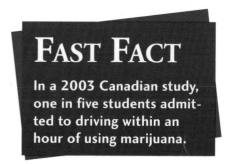

FAST FACT

In a 2003 Canadian study, one in five students admitted to driving within an hour of using marijuana.

Past Studies

A growing body of scientific evidence shows that drivers with modest amounts of THC in their system are no more dangerous than other drivers. A 2002 review of seven separate crash culpability studies involving 7,934 drivers reported, "Crash culpability studies [which attempt to correlate the responsibility of a driver for an accident to his or her consumption of a drug and the level of drug compound in his or her system] have failed to demonstrate that drivers with cannabinoids in the blood are significantly more likely than drug-free drivers to be culpable in road crashes."

Two other new accident studies have failed to find any hazard from marijuana. A study of 1500+ patients admitted to a Midwest trauma center published in the *Journal of Trauma Injury, Infection, and Critical*

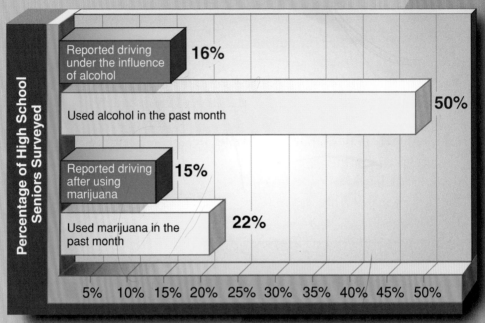

Teens' Use and Driving Under the Influence of Alcohol and Marijuana

Percentage of High School Seniors Surveyed

Reported driving under the influence of alcohol **16%**

Used alcohol in the past month **50%**

Reported driving after using marijuana **15%**

Used marijuana in the past month **22%**

5% 10% 15% 20% 25% 30% 35% 40% 45% 50%

Source: Trends in Lifetime Prevalence of Use of Various Drugs for Eighth, Tenth, and Twelfth Graders, Monitoring the Future Study, University of Michigan; O'Malley, Patrick and Johnston, Lloyd, "Unsafe Driving by High School Seniors: National Trends from 1976 to 2001 in Tickets and Accidents After Alcohol, Marijuana and Other Illegal Drugs," Journal of Studies on Alcohol (64: 305-12), May 2003.

Care found correlations between use of alcohol, cocaine and opiates with injuries. However, their data did not show "any statistically significant independent associations between injury and cannabis," researchers told NORML. . . .

Another study of road trauma from the Netherlands, which detected the presence of drugs through urine as well as blood tests, found significantly higher accident risks for alcohol and benzodiazepines (prescription tranquilizers) and less certain risks for amphetamines, cocaine and opiates, but no increased risk for cannabis.

In the largest U.S. survey of drug use and driving accidents to date, the National Highway Transportation Safety Administration [NHTSA] found that alcohol was by far the "dominant problem." At the same time it found "no indication that marijuana by itself was a cause of fatal accidents." The report was delayed and not publicized because it failed to confirm the expectations of administration drug warriors.

The NHTSA report did find that the combination of marijuana with alcohol and other drugs was highly dangerous. Similar results have been reported in other studies. For this reason, California NORML does not recommend permitting liquor sales on premises where marijuana is allowed.

Marijuana Versus Alcohol

On the other hand, studies have found that marijuana by itself tends to be significantly less dangerous than alcohol. A second NHTSA study of marijuana on actual driving performance found that the

This advertisment featuring New York mayor Michael Bloomberg was part of a 2002 campaign urging New York City to stop arresting and jailing people for smoking marijuana.

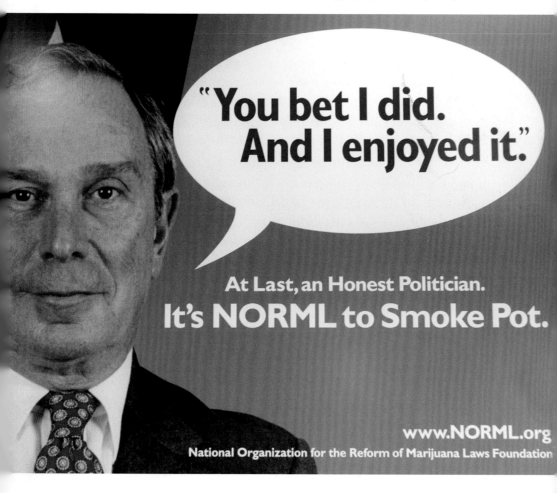

effects of THC appeared "relatively small" and less than those of drunken driving. It found that marijuana appeared to produce greater caution in drivers, apparently because users were more aware of their state and ready to compensate for it, whereas alcohol tended to encourage speeding and risky behavior. However, it also noted that marijuana could be dangerous in emergency situations that put high demands on drivers, or in combination with other drugs, especially alcohol.

High Doses of Marijuana

Other studies have shown that at sufficiently high doses marijuana does impair driving safety. Lab studies have demonstrated noticeable adverse effects for the first couple hours of intoxication, including impaired attention, unsteady lane control and following distance, and slower reaction time.

Most recently, a large-scale Australian accident survey found that drivers with higher THC blood levels—particularly those above 5 nanograms per milliliter (ng/ml) in plasma, indicating that the cannabis use had likely occurred within the past couple of hours—were correlated with a higher accident risk. However, THC levels below 5 ng/ml were associated with a lower risk than drug-free drivers.

Similar findings have been reported by an expert panel of the International Association of Cannabis Medicine charged with developing scientific per se standards for driving under the influence of marijuana. In its report, the panel concluded that THC blood plasma levels above 7–10 ng/ml might reasonably be taken as per se standards of impairment. It rejected lower blood level standards and standards based on urine metabolites as unsupported by the scientific evidence. However, it did suggest that lower THC blood limits might be appropriate where alcohol is also present.

Marijuana Not a Danger

In sum, current scientific evidence shows that the hazards of marijuana are dose-dependent, but generally less than those of alcohol. There is no evidence that marijuana has contributed signficantly to overall accident mortality. In fact, traffic accident mortality rates declined over the time when marijuana was first popularized in the 60s and 70s, and have continued to decline since.

EVALUATING THE AUTHOR'S ARGUMENTS:

The author says that very high doses of marijuana can be dangerous to driving. Does this strengthen or weaken his overall argument?

Chapter 2

Should Medical Marijuana Be Legalized?

Marijuana is prescribed by doctors for a variety of medicinal uses, a practice that is illegal at the federal level.

Medical Marijuana Helps Sick Patients

"Seventy-eight percent of Americans support 'making marijuana legally available . . . to reduce pain and suffering.'"

Medical Marijuana Policy Project

Marijuana is a safe and useful substance for alleviating symptoms related to cancer, multiple sclerosis, epilepsy, and many other conditions, according to the Marijuana Policy Project, the largest marijuana policy reform organization in the United States. Scientists have documented its therapeutic qualities, and the majority of Americans support the use of doctor-prescribed medicinal marijuana to ease the suffering of millions of people. However, the U.S. government has labeled marijuana as a dangerous drug with no accepted medical use. It remains illegal under federal law. The Marijuana Policy Project, which works to minimize the harm associated with marijuana, challenges government policy in its "Medical Marijuana Briefing Paper: The Need to Change State and Federal Law."

Medical Marijuana Policy Project, Medical Marijuana Briefing Paper 2005, Washington, DC: Marijuana Policy Project, 2006. Copyright © 2006 Marijuana Policy Project. All rights reserved. Reproduced by permission.

AS YOU READ, CONSIDER THE FOLLOWING QUESTIONS:
1. According to the article, what symptoms does marijuana alleviate?
2. How did the U.S. government schedule marijuana, and what does this mean?
3. Why is the Investigational New Drug (IND) program a failure?

For thousands of years, marijuana has been used to treat a wide variety of ailments. Until 1937, marijuana (*Cannabis sativa L.*) was legal in the United States for all purposes. Presently, federal law allows only seven Americans to use marijuana as a medicine.

On March 17, 1999, the National Academy of Sciences' Institute of Medicine (IOM) concluded that "there are some limited circumstances in which we recommend smoking marijuana for medical uses." The IOM report, the result of two years of research that was funded by the White House drug policy office, analyzed all existing data on marijuana's therapeutic uses. . . .

Marijuana Has Major Medicinal Value

Marijuana is one of the safest therapeutically active substances known. No one has ever died from an overdose, and it has a wide variety of therapeutic applications, including:

- Relief from nausea and appetite loss;
- Reduction of intraocular (within the eye) pressure;
- Reduction of muscle spasms; and
- Relief from chronic pain.

Marijuana is frequently beneficial in the treatment of the following conditions:

AIDS. Marijuana can reduce the nausea, vomiting, and loss of appetite caused by the ailment itself and by various AIDS medications.

Glaucoma. Marijuana can reduce intraocular pressure, alleviating the pain and slowing—and sometimes stopping—damage to the eyes. (Glaucoma is the leading cause of blindness in the United States. It damages vision by increasing eye pressure over time.)

Cancer. Marijuana can stimulate the appetite and alleviate nausea and vomiting, which are common side effects of chemotherapy treatment.

Multiple Sclerosis. Marijuana can limit the muscle pain and spasticity caused by the disease, as well as relieving tremor and unsteadiness of gait. (Multiple sclerosis is the leading cause of neurological disability among young and middle-aged adults in the United States.)

Epilepsy. Marijuana can prevent epileptic seizures in some patients.

Chronic Pain. Marijuana can alleviate the chronic, often debilitating pain caused by myriad disorders and injuries. Each of these applications has been deemed legitimate by at least one court, legislature, and/or government agency in the United States.

Many patients also report that marijuana is useful for treating arthritis, migraine, menstrual cramps, alcohol and opiate addiction, and depression and other debilitating mood disorders.

FAST FACT

Presently, patients can be arrested and sent to prison for using marijuana—even those who have a doctor's approval.

Marijuana could be helpful for millions of patients in the United States. Nevertheless, other than for the seven people with special permission from the federal government, medical marijuana remains illegal under federal law!

People currently suffering from any of the conditions mentioned above, for whom the legal medical options have proven unsafe or ineffective, have two options:

1. Continue to suffer without effective treatment; or
2. Illegally obtain marijuana—and risk suffering consequences directly related to its illegality, such as:
   - an insufficient supply due to the prohibition-inflated price or scarcity;
   - impure, contaminated, or chemically adulterated marijuana;
   - arrests, fines, court costs, property forfeiture, incarceration, probation, and criminal records.

The History of Medicinal Marijuana

Prior to 1937, at least 27 medicines containing marijuana were legally available in the United States. Many were made by well-known pharmaceutical firms that still exist today, such as Squibb (now Bristol-Myers Squibb) and Eli Lilly. The Marijuana Tax Act of 1937 federally prohibited marijuana. Dr. William C. Woodward of the American Medical Association opposed the Act, testifying that prohibition would ultimately prevent the medicinal uses of marijuana.

A woman smokes marijuana prescribed for her by a doctor. She has been using marijuana for more than four years for relief of pain from back and hip injuries.

The Controlled Substances Act of 1970 placed all illicit and prescription drugs into five "schedules" (categories). **Marijuana was placed in Schedule I, defining it as having a high potential for abuse, no currently accepted medical use in treatment in the United States, and a lack of accepted safety for use under medical supervision**.

This definition simply does not apply to marijuana. Of course, at the time of the Controlled Substances Act, marijuana had been prohibited for more than three decades. Its medicinal uses forgotten, marijuana was considered a dangerous and addictive narcotic.

A substantial increase in the number of recreational users in the 1970s contributed to the rediscovery of marijuana's medicinal uses:

- Many scientists studied the health effects of marijuana and inadvertently discovered marijuana's medicinal uses in the process.
- Many who used marijuana recreationally also suffered from diseases for which marijuana is beneficial. By accident, they discovered its therapeutic value.

As the word spread, more and more patients started self-medicating with marijuana. However, marijuana's Schedule I status bars doctors from prescribing it and severely curtails research.

The Struggle in Court

In 1972, a petition was submitted to the Bureau of Narcotics and Dangerous Drugs—now the Drug Enforcement Administration (DEA)—to reschedule marijuana to make it available by prescription.

After 16 years of court battles, the DEA's chief administrative law judge, Francis L. Young, ruled:

Marijuana, in its natural form, is one of the safest therapeutically active substances known. . . .

[T]he provisions of the [Controlled Substances] Act permit and require the transfer of marijuana from Schedule I to Schedule II.

It would be unreasonable, arbitrary and capricious for DEA to continue to stand between those sufferers and the benefits of this substance."

(September 6, 1988)

Marijuana's placement in Schedule II would enable doctors to prescribe it to their patients. **But top DEA bureaucrats rejected Judge Young's ruling and refused to reschedule marijuana**. Two appeals later, petitioners experienced their first defeat in the 22-year-old lawsuit. On February 18, 1994, the U.S. Court of Appeals (D.C. Circuit) ruled that the DEA is allowed to reject its judge's ruling and set its own criteria—enabling the DEA to keep marijuana in Schedule I.

However, Congress has the power to reschedule marijuana via legislation, regardless of the DEA's wishes.

Temporary Compassion

In 1975, Robert Randall, who suffered from glaucoma, was arrested for cultivating his own marijuana. He won his case by using the "medical necessity defense," forcing the government to find a way to provide him with his medicine. As a result, the Investigational New Drug (IND) compassionate access program was established, enabling some patients to receive marijuana from the government.

The program was grossly inadequate at helping the potentially millions of people who need medical marijuana. Many patients would never consider the idea that an illegal drug might be their best medicine, and most who were fortunate enough to discover marijuana's medicinal value did not discover the IND program. Those who did often could not find doctors willing to take on the program's arduous, bureaucratic requirements.

In 1992, in response to a flood of new applications from AIDS patients, the George H.W. Bush administration closed the program to new applicants, and pleas to reopen it were ignored by subsequent administrations. The IND program remains in operation only for the seven surviving, previously-approved patients.

Public and Professional Opinion

There is wide support for ending the prohibition of medical marijuana among both the public and the medical community:

- Since 1996, a majority of voters in Alaska, California, Colorado, the District of Columbia, Maine, Montana, Nevada, Oregon, and Washington state have voted in favor of ballot initiatives to remove criminal penalties for seriously ill people who grow or

Map of Medical Marijuana Resources

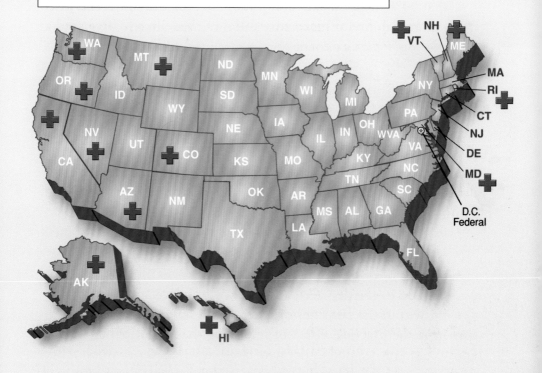

Source: NORML (National Organization for the Reform of Marijuana Laws) 2005.

possess medical marijuana. Polls have shown that public approval of these laws has increased since they went into effect.

- A national Gallup poll released November 1, 2005, found that 78% of Americans support "making marijuana legally available for doctors to prescribe in order to reduce pain and suffering." For over a decade, polls have consistently shown between 60% and 80% support for legal access to medical marijuana. Both a statewide Alabama poll commissioned by the *Mobile Register*, published in July 2004, and a November 2004 Scripps Howard Texas poll reported 75% support.

- Organizations supporting some form of physician supervised access to medical marijuana include the American Academy of Family Physicians, American Nurses Association, American Public Health Association, the *New England Journal of Medicine* and many others.

- A 1990 scientific survey of oncologists (cancer specialists) found that 54% of those with an opinion favored the controlled medical availability of marijuana and 44% had already suggested at least once that a patient obtain marijuana illegally. . . .

Changing State Laws

The federal government has no legal authority to prevent state governments from changing their laws to remove state-level criminal penalties for medical marijuana use. Hawaii enacted a medical marijuana law via its state legislature in 2000 and Vermont enacted a similar law in 2004. State legislatures have the authority and moral responsibility to change state law to:

- exempt seriously ill patients from state-level prosecution for medical marijuana possession and cultivation; and
- exempt doctors who recommend medical marijuana from prosecution or the denial of any right or privilege.

Even within the confines of federal law, states can enact reforms that have the practical effect of removing the fear of patients being arrested and prosecuted under state law—as well as the symbolic effect of pushing the federal government to allow doctors to prescribe marijuana.

U.S. Congress: The Final Battleground

State governments that want to allow marijuana to be sold in pharmacies have been stymied by the federal government's overriding prohibition of marijuana.

Patients' efforts to bring change through the federal courts have made little progress thus far. The U.S. Supreme Court's June 2005 decision in *Gonzales v. Raich* preserved state medical marijuana laws but allowed continued federal attacks on patients, even in states with such laws.

Efforts to obtain FDA [Food and Drug Administration] approval of marijuana also remain stalled. Though some small studies of marijuana are now underway, the National Institute on Drug Abuse—the only legal source of marijuana for clinical research in the U.S.—has consistently made it difficult (and often nearly impossible) for researchers to obtain marijuana for their studies. At present, it is effectively impossible to do the sort of large-scale, extremely costly trials required for FDA approval.

In the meantime, patients continue to suffer. **Congress has the power and the responsibility to change federal law so that seriously ill people nationwide can use medical marijuana without fear of arrest and imprisonment**.

EVALUATING THE AUTHORS' ARGUMENTS:

In the viewpoint you just read the authors argue that the majority of Americans and even most doctors favor the legalization of medicinal marijuana. If this is true, why does the government not make it easier for sick people to legally obtain and use marijuana? Even if medicinal marijuana is illegal under federal law, what can the states do? Do you see any potential problems with more lenient medicinal marijuana laws?

Viewpoint

2

Medical Marijuana Is Not Medicine

Karen P. Tandy

"Smoked marijuana is a health danger, not a cure."

According to a press release from the U.S. Drug Enforcement Administration (DEA), smoked marijuana is not medicine. Recent studies have proven that there is absolutely no medical value to marijuana for conditions related to AIDS, epilepsy, glaucoma, and other diseases. Not only can marijuana cause significant health problems such as chronic coughing, sneezing, chest colds, and bronchitis, it can lead to increased anxiety, depression, and a host of other ailments. According to the DEA in the article "Marijuana: The Myths Are Killing Us," marijuana is a dangerous drug with serious health, safety, social, academic, and economic consequences.

AS YOU READ, CONSIDER THE FOLLOWING QUESTIONS:

1. What support does the author offer for proving that marijuana has no medicinal value?
2. According to the author, in what ways is marijuana harmful to your health?
3. In what ways does marijuana use harm others besides the marijuana smoker?

Tandy, Karen P. From Police Chief Magazine, March, 2005. Copyright © 2003–2006 International Association of Chiefs of Police. All rights reserved. Reproduced by permission.

When 14-year-old Irma Perez of Belmont, California, took a single ecstasy pill one evening [in April 2004], she had no idea she would become one of the 26,000 people who die every year from drugs. Irma took ecstasy with two of her 14-year-old friends in her home. Soon after taking the tiny blue pill, Irma

Angel Raich speaks with reporters at her home in California in 2006. Raich sued then-U.S. attorney general John Ashcroft, asking for a court order allowing her to use marijuana for medical purposes.

complained of feeling awful and said she felt like she was "going to die." Instead of seeking medical care, her friends called the 17-year-old dealer who supplied the pills and asked for advice. The friends tried to get Irma to smoke marijuana, but when she couldn't because she was vomiting and lapsing into a coma, they stuffed marijuana leaves into her mouth because, according to news sources, "they knew that drug is sometimes used to treat cancer patients."

Irma Perez died from taking ecstasy, but compounding that tragedy was the deadly decision to use marijuana to "treat" her instead of making what could have been a lifesaving call to 911. Irma was a victim of our society's stunning misinformation about marijuana—a society that has come to believe that marijuana use is not only an individual's free choice but also is good medicine, a cure—all for a variety of ills. . . .

What is the antidote? Spreading the truth. As a prominent spokesperson in your community, you have the opportunity and, I

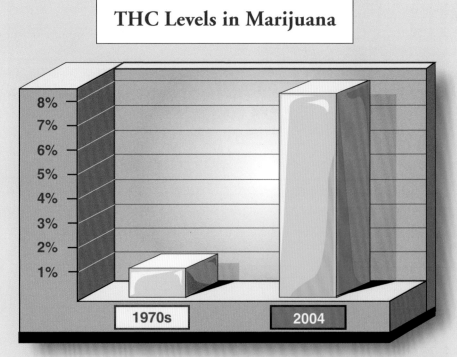

THC Levels in Marijuana

Source: White House Office of National Drug Control Policy (2004).

would argue, the responsibility to inform your neighbors. America is not suffering from anything that the truth can't cure. To help you set the record straight, this article seeks to rebut the rhetoric and recap the reality.

Smoked Marijuana Is Not Medicine

The scientific and medical communities have determined that smoked marijuana is a health danger, not a cure. There is no medical evidence that smoking marijuana helps patients. In fact, the Food and Drug Administration (FDA) has approved no medications that are smoked, primarily because smoking is a poor way to deliver medicine. Morphine, for example has proven to be a medically valuable drug, but the FDA does not endorse smoking opium or heroin.

Congress enacted laws against marijuana in 1970 based in part on its conclusion that marijuana has no scientifically proven medical value, which the U.S. Supreme Court affirmed more than 30 years later in *United States v. Oakland Cannabis Buyers' Cooperative, et al.,* 532 U.S. 483 (2001). Marijuana remains in schedule 1 of the Controlled Substances Act because it has a high potential for abuse, a lack of accepted safety for use under medical supervision, and no currently accepted medical value.

The American Medical Association has rejected pleas to endorse marijuana as medicine, and instead urged that marijuana remain a prohibited schedule 1 drug at least until the results of controlled studies are in. The National Multiple Sclerosis Society stated that studies done to date "have not provided convincing evidence that marijuana benefits people with MS" and does not recommend it as a treatment. Further, the MS Society states that for people with MS "long-term use of marijuana may be associated with significant serious side effects."

The British Medical Association has taken a similar position, voicing "extreme concern" that downgrading the criminal status of marijuana would "mislead" the public into thinking that the drug is safe to use when, "in fact, it has been linked to greater risk of heart disease, lung cancer, bronchitis, and emphysema."

In 1999 the Institute of Medicine (IOM) undertook a landmark study reviewing the alleged medical properties of marijuana. Advocates of so-called medical marijuana frequently tout this study, but the study's findings decisively undercut their arguments. In truth, the IOM explicitly found that marijuana is not medicine and expressed concern about patients' smoking it because smoking is a harmful drug-delivery system. The IOM further found that there was no scientific evidence that smoked marijuana had medical value, even for the chronically ill, and concluded that "there is little future in smoked marijuana as a medically approved medication." In fact, the researchers who conducted the study could find no medical value to marijuana for virtually any ailment they examined, including the treatment of wasting syndrome in AIDS patients, movement disorders such as Parkinson's disease and epilepsy, or glaucoma. . . .

Liberalization of Drug Laws in Other Countries Has Often Resulted in Higher Use of Dangerous Drugs

Over the past decade, drug policy in some foreign countries, particularly those in Europe, has gone through some dramatic changes toward greater liberalization with failed results. Consider the experience of the Netherlands, where the government reconsidered its legalization measures in light of that country's experience. After marijuana use became legal, consumption nearly tripled among 18- to 20-year-olds. As awareness of the harm of marijuana grew, the number of cannabis coffeehouses in the Netherlands decreased 36 percent in six years. Almost all Dutch towns have a cannabis policy, and 73 percent of them have a no-tolerance policy toward the coffeehouses.

In 1987 Swiss officials permitted drug use and sales in a Zurich park, which was soon dubbed Needle Park, and Switzerland became a magnet for drug users the world over. Within five years, the number of regular drug users at the park had reportedly swelled from a few hundred to 20,000. The area around the park became crime-ridden to the point that the park had to be shut down and the experiment terminated.

Marijuana use by Canadian teenagers is at a 25-year peak in the wake of an aggressive decriminalization movement. At the very time a decriminalization bill was before the House of Commons, the Canadian government released a report showing that marijuana smoking among teens is "at levels that we haven't seen since the late '70s when rates reached their peak." After a large decline in the 1980s,

The prescription-grade marijuana offered for sale by the Cannabis Club in San Francisco, c. 1997, came in a variety of forms: cakes, cookies, and other treats.

marijuana use among teens increased during the 1990s, as young people apparently became "confused about the state of federal pot laws."

Marijuana Is Dangerous to the User

Use of marijuana has adverse health, safety, social, academic, economic, and behavioral consequences; and children are the most vulnerable to its damaging effects. Marijuana is the most widely used illicit drug in America and is readily available to kids. Compounding the problem is that the marijuana of today is not the marijuana of the baby boomers 30 years ago. Average THC levels rose from less than 1 percent in the mid-1970s to more than 8 percent in 2004. And the potency of B.C. Bud, a popular type of marijuana cultivated in British

Columbia, Canada, is roughly twice the national average—ranging from 15 percent THC content to 20 percent or even higher.

Marijuana use can lead to dependence and abuse. Marijuana was the second most common illicit drug responsible for drug treatment admissions in 2002—outdistancing crack cocaine, the next most prevalent cause. Shocking to many is that more teens are in treatment each year for marijuana dependence than for alcohol and all other illegal drugs combined. This is a trend that has been increasing for more than a decade: in 2002, 64 percent of adolescent treatment admissions reported marijuana as their primary substance of abuse, compared to 23 percent in 1992.

Marijuana is a gateway drug. In drug law enforcement, rarely do we meet heroin or cocaine addicts who did not start their drug use with marijuana. Scientific studies bear out our anecdotal findings. For example, the *Journal of the American Medical Association* reported, based on a study of 300 sets of twins, that marijuana-using twins were four times more likely than their siblings to use cocaine and crack cocaine, and five times more likely to use hallucinogens such as LSD. Furthermore, the younger a person is when he or she first uses marijuana, the more likely that person is to use cocaine and heroin and become drug-dependent as an adult. One study found that 62 percent of the adults who first tried marijuana before they were 15 were likely to go on to use cocaine. In contrast, only 1 percent or less of adults who never tried marijuana used heroin or cocaine.

Smoking marijuana can cause significant health problems. Marijuana contains more than 400 chemicals, of which 60 are cannabinoids. Smoking a marijuana cigarette deposits about three to five times more tar into the lungs than one filtered tobacco cigarette. Consequently, regular marijuana smokers suffer from many of the same health problems as tobacco smokers, such as chronic coughing and wheezing, chest colds, and chronic bronchitis. In fact, studies show that smoking three to four joints per day causes at least as much harm to the respiratory system as smoking a full pack of cigarettes every day. Marijuana smoke also contains 50 to 70 percent more carcinogenic hydrocarbons than tobacco smoke and produces high levels of an enzyme that converts certain hydrocarbons into malignant cells.

In addition, smoking marijuana can lead to increased anxiety, panic attacks, depression, social withdrawal, and other mental health problems, particularly for teens. Research shows that kids aged 12 to 17 who smoke marijuana weekly are three times more likely than nonusers to have suicidal thoughts. Marijuana use also can cause cognitive impairment, to include such short-term effects as distorted perception, memory loss, and trouble with thinking and problem solving. Students with an average grade of D or below were found to be more than four times as like-

FAST FACT

The American Medical Association has rejected pleas to endorse smoked marijuana as medicine.

ly to have used marijuana in the past year as youths who reported an average grade of A. For young people, whose brains are still developing, these effects are particularly problematic and jeopardize their ability to achieve their full potential.

Marijuana Use Harms Nonusers

We need to put to rest the thought that there is such a thing as a lone drug user, a person whose habits affect only himself or herself. Drug use, including marijuana use, is not a victimless crime. Some in your communities may resist involvement because they think someone else's drug use is not hurting them. But this kind of not-my-problem thinking is tragically misguided. Ask those same people about secondhand smoke from cigarettes, and they'll quickly acknowledge the harm that befalls nonsmokers. Secondhand smoke is a well-known problem, one that Americans are becoming more unwilling to bear. We need to apply the same common-sense thinking to the even more pernicious secondhand effects of drug use.

Take for instance the disastrous effects of marijuana smoking on driving. As the National Highway Traffic Safety Administration (NHTSA) noted, "Epidemiology data from . . . traffic arrests and fatalities indicate that after alcohol, marijuana is the most frequently detected psychoactive substance among driving populations." Marijuana causes drivers to experience decreased car handling performance, increased reaction times, distorted time and distance estimation, sleepiness, impaired motor skills, and lack of concentration.

The extent of the problem of marijuana-impaired driving is startling. One in six (or 600,000) high school students drive under the influence of marijuana, almost as many as drive under the influence of alcohol, according to estimates released in September 2003 by the Office of National Drug Control Policy (ONDCP). A study of motorists pulled over for reckless driving showed that, among those who were not impaired by alcohol, 45 percent tested positive for marijuana.

Speed Bump © 2004 Dave Coverly. All rights reserved. Used with the permission of Dave Coverly in conjunction with the Cartoonist Group.

For those of you who patrol streets and highways, you know that the consequences of marijuana-impaired driving can be tragic. For example, four children and their van driver—nicknamed Smokey by the children for his regular marijuana smoking—died in April 2002 when a Tippy Toes Learning Academy van veered off a freeway and hit a concrete bridge abutment. He was found at the crash scene with marijuana in his pocket.

EVALUATING THE AUTHOR'S ARGUMENTS:

In the viewpoint you just read the author compares smoking marijuana to smoking tobacco. Do you think that smoking marijuana is more harmful than smoking tobacco? Why or why not?

Legalizing Medical Marijuana Will Result in Increased Recreational Use

"Liberalization of marijuana policy will send a false and misleading message that marijuana is harmless."

Mark R. Trouville

Legalizing medicinal marijuana is a dangerous decision with serious ramifications for law enforcement, drug trafficking, and public health, according to testimony delivered before the Vermont House Committee on Health and Welfare. The absence of state penalties for medical marijuana will spike recreational use, encouraging flagrant violations of federal law and introducing the drug to even more young people. Moreover, long-time drug dealers will be able to pose as "caregivers," selling thousands of dollars in "medicine" to their "patients," thus creating a logistical nightmare for law enforcement officers. The states should not attempt to legalize a harmful, dangerous substance

Trouville, Mark R. DEA Congressional Testimony, U.S. Drug Enforcement Administration, 2004.

deemed illegal under federal law, according to Mark R. Trouville, special agent in charge of the New England field division of the Drug Enforcement Administration.

AS YOU READ, CONSIDER THE FOLLOWING QUESTIONS:
1. According to the author, what has happened in states where medicinal marijuana was legalized?
2. How will legalizing medical marijuana undermine the efforts of law enforcement officers, according to Trouville?
3. What kind of message will liberalizing marijuana laws send to the public, according to the author?

The overwhelming weight of evidence and experience conclusively show that marijuana and its consequences are dangerous to both users and non-users. The Drug Enforcement Administration (DEA) therefore vigilantly enforces federal laws prohibiting manufacturing and distribution of marijuana. We believe that the proposal before you today would have a significant negative impact on federal enforcement. It is not only inconsistent with federal law, it obstructs federal law. We have seen from experience in other states that state laws permitting use of marijuana encourage violations of federal law and pose significant practical obstacles to law enforcement. Moreover, we do not believe that the proposal will accomplish its stated goals because, as the Institute of Medicine (IOM) put it, "[t]here is little future in smoked marijuana as a medically approved medication." On balance, the potentially significant negative impact on public health and safety as well as law enforcement should weigh heavily against this legislation. We believe the citizens of Vermont will be best served by keeping state law consistent with the view Congress has settled upon based on the weight of scientific and medical evidence.

Increased Use

While states are free to define criminal acts and impose corresponding penalties in the manner they see fit, it does not follow that the absence of state penalties "legalizes" conduct that remains unlawful under federal law. More than seven years of experience have demonstrated that when a state legalizes marijuana under its law, residents are effectively encouraged to violate federal drug laws. This result undermines the protection to the public health and safety inherent in the federal drug approval process, creates public confusion, interferes with law enforcement efforts to combat drug trafficking, and runs afoul of the Supremacy Clause of the United States Constitution.

A girl smokes marijuana on the tour plane of the 1960s rock band the Monkees. Recreational marijuana use was prevalent during that time period.

This is not rhetoric—let me illustrate these very real problems from the DEA's experience in other states. For example, two investigations involving "medical" marijuana clubs demonstrate that purported "medical" use only hides everyday drug dealing. The clubs' owners cultivated and distributed significant amounts of "medical" marijuana in the area, not only to "patients," but to anyone who wanted to buy it. In one of the investigations, a witness claims to have seen more than 4,000 plants being cultivated inside one of the clubs. In the second case, approximately 979 plants and several pounds of processed marijuana were seized during the execution of a Federal search warrant. One of the owners admitted that he rented the property and grew the marijuana for his 120 "patients." In addition to the contraband that was seized, documents indicating that the grower had made $140,000 in profits from his drug dealing were also seized.

Violating Federal Law

Along these lines, I would like to point out that the bill before you today is conspicuously silent with regard to the fact that the cultivation, distribution, and possession of marijuana, even in compliance with the bill, would violate federal law and subject the individuals engaged in such conduct to criminal and civil prosecution. That omission points to a glaring practical issue in the legislation—there is simply no way for it to be given effect without encouraging and facilitating trafficking in a federally controlled substance.

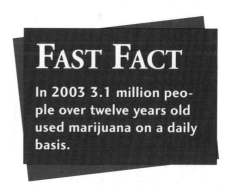

FAST FACT

In 2003 3.1 million people over twelve years old used marijuana on a daily basis.

When the General Assembly considers this proposal, we hope it will consider how these types of laws undermine the efforts of law enforcement officials at every level nationwide. In the states that have passed these types of laws since 1996, longtime drug dealers have reinvented themselves as "caregivers" so that they can claim immunity from prosecution. This proposal and similar laws enacted in other states are written in a manner that makes it easy for any drug dealer to concoct a "medical" marijuana defense.

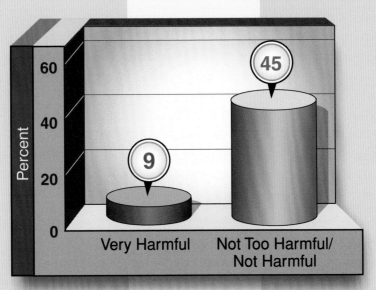

Teens Who Believe Marijuana Is Not Harmful Are Five Times Likelier to Smoke Pot than Teens Who Believe Marijuana Is Very Harmful

Source: CASA, 2003.

The impact on law enforcement should be obvious, as a Maryland lawyer recently was publicly quoted as saying there "are a whole bunch of people who like marijuana who can now try to use this defense."

Sending the Wrong Message

The DEA vigilantly enforces federal laws against marijuana trafficking for a simple reason that remains as compelling, if not more compelling, today than in the past: marijuana use is dangerous to both the user and the non-user, particularly children. This is true irrespective of whether or not its use is for purported "medical" purposes. While the list of these concerns is lengthy, I would like to highlight the most telling examples.

Marijuana is the most widely used illicit drug in America and a widespread social and human service concern. More young people are currently in treatment for marijuana dependency than for alcohol and all other illegal drugs combined, and mentions of marijuana use in emergency room visits have risen 176 percent since 1994, surpassing those of heroin. Any liberalization of marijuana policy will send a false and misleading message that marijuana is harmless if not affirmatively good for you, exacerbating the already significant problem of marijuana abuse. Use of marijuana by young people is a frequent precursor to the use of more dangerous drugs, and signals a significantly enhanced likelihood of drug problems in adult life. For example, a study done by the Substance Abuse and Mental Health Services Administration (SAMHSA) in 2002 found that 62 percent of the adults who first tried marijuana before they were 15 years old were likely to go on to cocaine—but the same was true of only one-half of one percent of adults who had never tried marijuana.

Dangerous and Deadly

Smoked marijuana is also dangerous to those who use it, belying any beneficent rationale in permitting its use. Marijuana smoke contains 50 percent to 70 percent more carcinogenic hydrocarbons than tobacco smoke. Marijuana may promote cancer of the respiratory tract and provide heightened risk of lung infection and many other diseases. The British Medical Association (BMA) is so concerned about the negative health impact of liberalization initiatives such as the one before you today that it recently voiced "extreme concern" that altering the criminal penalties for marijuana use would create a misleading impression that marijuana is safe to use that the BMA emphasized that "the public must be made aware of the harmful effects we know result from smoking the drug."

EVALUATING THE AUTHOR'S ARGUMENTS:

According to the author, what problems occur when marijuana is illegal under federal law, but legalized under state law? Why is this a bad idea?

Viewpoint
4

Legalizing Medical Marijuana Will Not Result in Increased Recreational Use

"Enactment of state medical marijuana laws does not increase teen marijuana use."

Karen O'Keefe and Mitch Earleywine

Government organizations claim legalizing medical marijuana sends the wrong message to the public and will result in increased recreational use, especially among youth. According to a recent report, *Marijuana Use by Young People: The Impact of State Medical Marijuana Laws*, nothing could be further from the truth. In this report authors Karen O'Keefe of the Marijuana Policy Project and Mitch Earleywine from the University of Albany analyze data from ten states with medical marijuana laws. This data suggests that enacting medical marijuana laws does not increase recreational use, and instead,

O'Keefe, Karen, Esq., Mitch Earleywine, PhD. From *Marijuana Use by Young People: The Impact of State Medical Marijuana Laws*, Washington, DC: Marijuana Policy Project, 2006. Copyright © 2006 Marijuana Policy Project. All rights reserved. Reproduced by permission.

results in a modest *decline* in marijuana use. Moreover, research shows no support for the "wrong message" effect, undermining an important argument used by opponents of medical marijuana.

AS YOU READ, CONSIDER THE FOLLOWING QUESTIONS:
1. According to the authors, what was the impact of the passage of the nation's first state medical marijuana law?
2. According to the authors, what may be a reason for the decline in marijuana use after the passage of medical marijuana laws?
3. According to the authors, what should legislators do as they consider medical marijuana proposals?

The debate over medical marijuana laws has included extensive discussion of whether such laws "send the wrong message to young people," thus increasing teen marijuana use. This is the first report to analyze all available data to determine the trends in teen marijuana use in states that have passed medical marijuana laws.

Nine years after the passage of the nation's first state medical marijuana law, California's Prop. 215, a considerable body of data shows that no state with a medical marijuana law has experienced an increase in youth marijuana use since their law's enactment. All have reported overall decreases—exceeding 50% in some age groups—strongly suggesting that enactment of state medical marijuana laws does not increase teen marijuana use.

FAST FACT

In Washington State, sixth graders' current and lifetime marijuana use dropped by at least 50 percent since the 1998 enactment of the state's medical marijuana law.

No Increased Use of Marijuana
- In *California*—which has the longest-term, most detailed data available—the number of ninth graders reporting marijuana use

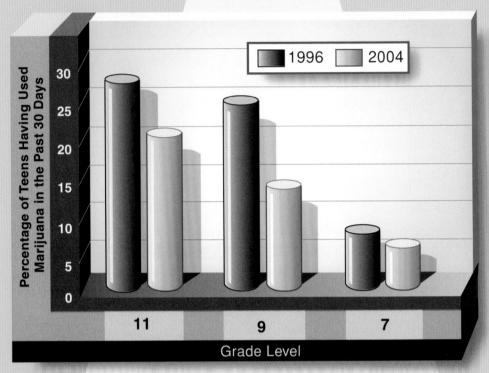

Source: Medical Marijuana Policy Project, 2006.

in the last 30 days declined by 47% from 1996 (when the state's medical marijuana law passed) to 2004. An analysis commissioned by the California Department of Alcohol and Drug Programs found "no evidence supporting that the passage of Proposition 215 increased marijuana use during this period."

- In *Washington* state, sixth graders' current and lifetime marijuana use has dropped by at least 50% since the 1998 enactment of the state's medical marijuana law. All other surveyed grade levels have seen both lifetime and current marijuana use drop by between 25% and 50%.
- In *Hawaii,* youth marijuana use has decreased among all surveyed grade levels—by as much as 38%—since the 2000 passage of the state's medical marijuana law.

- Data from *Maine* suggest a modest decline since the 1999 passage of its law. Data from *Nevada* (whose law was passed in 2000) and *Alaska* (whose law was passed in 1998) show overall decreases in marijuana use, with a modest increase in a few individual grade levels. Data from *Oregon* (whose law passed in 1998) suggest modest declines in marijuana use among the two grades surveyed in 2004, a slight decrease in lifetime marijuana use among high schoolers, and a tiny increase in current marijuana use among high schoolers. *Colorado* (whose law passed in 2000) is the only state without an in-depth statewide survey, but the limited data available suggest modest declines in Colorado teens' marijuana usage as well.
- *Vermont* and *Montana*, whose medical marijuana laws were enacted in 2004, have not yet produced statistically valid data covering the period since their laws were passed.
- *Nationwide*, teenage marijuana use has decreased in the nine years since California enacted the country's first effective medical

An eighty-two-year-old medical marijuana patient takes part in a 2002 protest against raids and arrests at state-approved and licensed medical marijuana dispensaries in California.

marijuana law. Overall, the trends in states with medical marijuana laws are slightly more favorable than the trends nationwide. California, Washington, and Colorado have all seen much greater drops in marijuana usage than have occurred nationwide. Overall, Alaska's and Hawaii's trends are also more favorable than nationwide trends, though some individual measures are less favorable. Trends from Maine, Oregon, and Nevada are slightly less favorable than nationwide trends, although use is still down. . . .

Conclusions and Recommendations

Since the mid-1990s, the U.S. has witnessed a well-publicized and sometimes emotional national debate over the medical use of marijuana. Contrary to the fears expressed by opponents of medical marijuana laws, there is no evidence that the enactment of 10 state medical marijuana laws has produced an increase in adolescent marijuana use in those states or nationwide. Instead, data from those states suggest a modest decline overall, with very large declines in some age

Signe Wilkinson's Editorial Cartoon © 2005 Signe Wilkinson. All rights reserved. Used with permission of Signe Wilkinson and the Washington Post Writers Group in conjunction with the Cartoonist Group. Printed originally in the Philadelphia Daily News.

groups in some states. Overall, the decrease in teen marijuana use in medical marijuana states has slightly exceeded the national decline.

In all eight states with available data covering two or more years since enactment of their medical marijuana laws, teen marijuana use declined overall, sometimes dramatically, after passage of a medical marijuana law. Only Hawaii had any data suggesting an overall increase since its law's passage, and making year-to-year comparisons before and after the relevant 2002 survey is considered invalid by the commissioning organization, the NSDUH [National Survey on Drug Use and Health]. Further, far more comprehensive data show decreases among all surveyed ages of Hawaiian youth.

While it is not possible with existing data to determine conclusively that state medical marijuana laws caused the documented declines in adolescent marijuana use, the overwhelming downward trend strongly suggests that the effect of state medical marijuana laws on teen marijuana use has been either neutral or positive, discouraging youthful experimentation with the drug. California researchers, who appear to be the only ones to specifically study the issue in the context of a survey of adolescent drug use, found no evidence of a "wrong message" effect. The reasons for this lack of impact have not been adequately studied. Perhaps medical marijuana laws send a very different message than opponents of such laws have suggested: Marijuana is a treatment for serious illness, not a toy, and requires cautious and careful handling. Legislators considering medical marijuana proposals should evaluate the bills on their own merits, without concern for unproven claims that such laws increase teen marijuana use. Opponents of medical marijuana laws should cease making such unsubstantiated claims.

EVALUATING THE AUTHORS' ARGUMENTS:

This article provides a lot of data to debunk the "wrong message" argument employed by medical marijuana opponents. Do you think this article is convincing? Should legislators continue to use the "wrong message" argument? Why or why not?

Chapter 3

Are Marijuana Drug Policies Fair?

Marijuana laws are debated at both the state and federal levels.

Viewpoint

1

Prison Time for Minor Offenders Is a Problem

Ryan S. King and Marc Mauer

"One in four persons in prison for a marijuana offense can be classified as a low-level offender."

The war on drugs focuses disproportionately on low-level marijuana possession charges, putting thousands of minor offenders behind bars. In fact, one in four of those in prison for marijuana offenses is classified as a low-level offender. In the report *The War on Marijuana: The Transformation of the War on Drugs in the 1990s* authors Ryan S. King and Marc Mauer challenge the way the criminal justice system treats marijuana offenders. According to the authors, billions of dollars are spent every year in the overzealous arrest, prosecution, and incarceration of casual marijuana users. The authors work for the Sentencing Project, a national nonprofit organization engaged in research and advocacy on criminal justice policy issues.

AS YOU READ, CONSIDER THE FOLLOWING QUESTIONS:

1. According to the authors, what do some states mandate for first-time marijuana possession?

King, Ryan S., and Marc Mauer. From *The War on Marijuana: The Transformation of the War on Drugs in the 1990s*, Washington, DC: The Sentencing Project, 2005. Copyright © 2005 by The Sentencing Project. Reproduced by permission.

In 2000, persons convicted of felony marijuana offenses were likely to be incarcerated. Half (51%) of the convictions for possession led to a prison or jail term, as did two-thirds (63%) of the trafficking convictions. Overall, one-third of all felony marijuana convictions resulted in a prison term of at least one year. This rate was the same for both marijuana trafficking and possession. [Marijuana trafficking involves the manufacturing, sales, distribution, possession with intent to sell, or smuggling of marijuana. Possession refers to the owning, holding or having any amount of marijuana.]. . .

Conventional wisdom suggests that individuals sentenced to prison for possession are repeat offenders with significant criminal histories. Although this may be true of many sentences, some states mandate incarceration even for some types of first-time marijuana possession. . . .

Average Sentence Length Two Years

Recent data on sentence length indicates that persons sentenced for a marijuana felony are likely to face sentences in the range of the national average for aggravated assault. In 2000, the average sentence for a person convicted of aggravated assault in a state court and sentenced to incarceration (prison or jail) was 37 months, while the average sentence for persons sentenced to probation for a felony was 40 months. An analysis of those figures for persons sentenced for marijuana felonies indicate a similar sentencing range. The average sentence for persons convicted of a marijuana felony in state court in 2000 was 28 months for incarceration and 40 months for probation. . . .

Separated by type of marijuana offense, we find that possession cases actually result in more severe sentences than trafficking. Persons sentenced for trafficking received an average of 27 months incarceration, while those sentenced to probation received 39 months. For possession, the incarceration average was 31 months and the probation average was 42 months. . . .

The Cost to Law Enforcement

The relatively stable patterns in state court conviction data, in light of the growth in arrests, raises questions about the allocation of law enforcement resources during the 1990s. While the numbers of arrests have more than doubled, making marijuana the single most pursued offense by American law enforcement agents, overall felony convictions have increased only modestly during the decade. Further, there is no discernable increase in the severity of marijuana offenses, since similar proportions are being sentenced to prison as in the past. Therefore, it appears that the court system is expending resources processing, dismissing, and filtering the increasing wave of marijuana arrestees. We estimate that 3.6% ($1.36 billion) of the national judicial and legal budget for 2001 ($37.8 billion) was spent on the court processing of marijuana offenders. The fact that the upward trend in arrests is not reflected in felony conviction data suggests that the quality of arrests has diminished greatly. It is reasonable to surmise that

Source: FBI's Division of Uniform Crime Reports, *Crime in the United States: 2003*, published in October 2004.

the growth in marijuana arrests, which are primarily for possession, is laden with misdemeanor charges and cases that are dismissed by the prosecuting authority. From a policy standpoint, the question is whether this is an efficient use of law enforcement and court system resources. . . .

Marijuana and the Correctional System

The endpoint in the criminal justice system is corrections, where persons sentenced to supervision are either incarcerated in prison or jail, or in the community on probation or parole. Based on current prison population counts, we estimate that there are 27,900 persons in state and federal prison serving a sentence for which a marijuana violation

A young woman is stopped by authorities after buying a joint from a man driving an ice-cream truck.

is the controlling (or most serious) offense. This translates to a national estimated loss of more than $600 million per year. Twenty-three percent of marijuana offenders are incarcerated for a possession offense, 15% for possession with intent to distribute, and 59% for trafficking. Of the total, 40% are incarcerated for the first time, 48% are recidivists with no current or prior violent offense history, and 12% are recidivists with a past violent offense in their criminal history. . . .

This initial analysis raises questions about the severity of offenders incarcerated in state and federal prisons for marijuana offenses. Nearly 90% have no history of a violent offense.

FAST FACT

Each year more than 650,000 Americans are arrested on minor marijuana possession charges.

However, violent offenses are not the only measure of a person's risk to society. Many officials assert that prison sentences for marijuana are imposed for high level offenses. In order to address this question, we analyzed the data from the *Survey of Inmates* on offender role in a drug enterprise.

The *Inmate Survey* asks respondents to report their activity in the drug trade. Although self-report data suffers from some inherent biases, it is a much better indicator of individual level drug involvement because, unlike the controlling offense, it is not impacted by pre-trial discretion and negotiations regarding charging level (as discussed in the section on court processes). We define drug activity as high-level if the individual has been involved in "importing," "manufacturing," "money laundering" or "distribution to other sellers." We estimate that 48% of marijuana offenders in state and federal prison were engaged in high-level drug activity prior to their arrest. Federal marijuana offenders participated in high-level activity at a higher rate (65%) than state prisoners (40%).

Using reported activity response as an indicator, there is reason to question the assertion that only serious marijuana distributors are incarcerated in prison. In fact, the data strongly indicate that a significant number of marijuana offenders are in prison for playing a low-level role in the drug market. We can see this by identifying only those persons in state or federal prison on a first-time offense, who had not played a role of importer, manufacturer, or distributor of marijuana, and who did not involve a weapon in their offense. . . . When these characteristics are taken into consideration, there are still 6,600 (24%) marijuana offenders in prison for a low-level offense. Based upon these criteria, we conclude that at least one in four persons in prison for a marijuana offense can be classified as a low-level offender.

EVALUATING THE AUTHORS' ARGUMENTS:

The authors seem to suggest that law enforcement efforts and taxpayer dollars could be better spent on activities other than the arrest and prosecution of minor marijuana offenders. Do you agree with this argument? Why or why not?

Viewpoint 2

Prison Time for Minor Offenders Is Not a Problem

John P. Walters

> *"There's very little chance that anyone in this country . . . will be sent to prison for merely puffing a 'joint.'"*

Marijuana legalization advocates paint a bleak picture for marijuana smokers, claiming that even first-time offenders end up in prison. In reality, only about 0.7 percent of the state inmate population is imprisoned simply for marijuana possession, according to recent studies. The vast majority of offenders incarcerated for marijuana are found guilty of trafficking or violating parole, have criminal histories, or were arrested for possession in a drug-free zone, such as a school. According to a recent report by John P. Walters, director of the Office of National Drug Control Policy, the way the criminal justice system handles marijuana-related offenses is fair and equitable; prisons are not overflowing with people arrested just for smoking pot. In his report *Who's Really in Prison for Marijuana?* Walters attempts to set the record straight.

Walters, John. *Who's Really in Prison for Marijuana?*, Office of National Drug Control Policy, 2004.

AS YOU READ, CONSIDER THE FOLLOWING QUESTIONS:
1. According to Walters, who is responsible for perpetuating the myth that prisons are packed with offenders for simple marijuana possession?
2. According to recent data, what percentage of state inmates are jailed for a first-time marijuana offense?
3. How much marijuana would have to be involved to generate a $4 million fine and a life sentence?

T he idea that our nation's prisons are overflowing with otherwise law-abiding people convicted for nothing more than simple possession of marijuana is treated by many as conventional wisdom.

But this, in fact, is a myth—an illusion conjured and aggressively perpetuated by drug advocacy groups seeking to relax or abolish America's marijuana laws. In reality, the vast majority of inmates in state and federal prison for marijuana have been found guilty of much more than simple possession. Some were convicted for drug trafficking, some for marijuana possession along with one or more other offenses. And many of those serving time for marijuana pled down to possession in order to avoid prosecution on much more serious charges.

Debunking Myths

In 1997, the year for which the most recent data are available, just 1.6 percent of the state inmate population were held for offenses involving *only* marijuana, and less than one percent of all state prisoners (0.7 percent) were incarcerated with marijuana *possession* as the only charge, according to the U.S. Department of Justice's Bureau of Justice Statistics (BJS). An even smaller fraction of state prisoners in 1997 who were convicted just for marijuana possession were first-time offenders (0.3 percent).

The numbers on the federal level tell a similar story. Out of all drug defendants sentenced in federal court for marijuana crimes in 2001, the overwhelming majority were convicted for *trafficking*, according to the U.S. Sentencing Commission. Only 2.3 percent—186 people—received sentences for simple possession, and of the 174 for whom sentencing information is known, just 63 actually served time behind bars.

Drug use harms the user and it harms the community, and because of this, criminal penalties have been put in place to control the possession and use of illicit substances. Built into the criminal justice system is an appropriate measure of discretion that responds to the gravity of the offense. Those who persistently violate the country's drug laws face criminal penalties, which may include time behind bars. For offenders whose involvement in law-breaking is minor, the sanctions are slight and often involve a referral to treatment rather than incarceration.

And yet, in spite of these facts, a false characterization continues to be promoted that depicts the criminal-justice response to marijuana violations as unduly harsh, exclusively punitive, and disproportionate. This characterization must be countered by the truth, which is this: Americans are not routinely being sent to prison in large numbers just for possessing small amounts of marijuana. Our criminal justice system, on the whole, is fair and equitable, and despite frequent claims to the contrary, there's very little chance that anyone in this country, particularly a first-time offender, will be sent to prison for merely puffing a "joint.". . .

FAST FACT

Less than 1 percent of state prison inmates in 1997 were serving time just for marijuana possession.

Beyond the Claims

It would be wrong to suggest that simple-possession offenders *never* see the inside of a prison cell. Sometimes they do, of course. A few may be sentenced outright, even when no other charges or aggravating factors are involved. But there is also a range of other circumstances under which a simple-possession marijuana offender might receive a prison sentence. For example, this could happen if:

- the marijuana offense was committed while the offender was on probation or parole;
- an offender charged with a more serious crime pleads guilty to

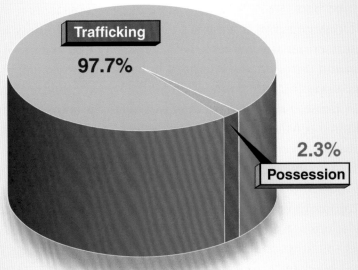

Marijuana Convictions in 2001

Trafficking

97.7%

2.3%
Possession

Source: Office of National Drug Control Policy, 2004.

the lesser offense of marijuana possession but, as part of a plea bargain, is required to serve a prison sentence;

- the offender has a criminal history, particularly one involving drugs or violent crime;
- the violation took place in a designated drug-free zone (such as on school property); or
- the marijuana sentence piggybacks (runs concurrent with) the sentence for one or more other offenses.

Despite overwhelming evidence to the contrary, there is no shortage of claims about so-called victims of the drug war who, charged with nothing more than minor marijuana violations, are serving long prison terms. Some of these allegations are grounded in truth but lack crucial elaboration or context. Most are exaggerations or blatant fiction. . . .

The Claim:

- "There have been 13,000,000 marijuana-related arrests since 1970."
- "In all, 704,812 Americans were arrested last year on marijuana-related charges."
- "800,000 people are arrested on marijuana charges each year."
- "5.2 million marijuana arrests since 1992."

Look Again:

It's true that many people are arrested for offenses involving marijuana. However, the above assertions are vague and misleading, in that "marijuana-related arrests," "marijuana-related charges," "marijuana charges," and "marijuana arrests" do not distinguish between a college student caught with one joint and a trafficker with several tons. Nor do they reflect how many of those arrests involved other, more serious crimes, or how many of those arrests actually led to incarceration.

The Claim:

"The penalties for a first pot offense range from probation to life in prison and fines of up to $4 million, depending on the amount of pot."

Look Again:

The probation part of that statement is correct. The part about life in prison and a $4 million fine evidently comes from the Federal Sentencing Guidelines for the sale or cultivation of enormous amounts of marijuana. To generate a life sentence in federal court, a conviction would have to involve at least 33 *tons* of marijuana and additional aggravating factors, such as a leadership role in a continuing criminal activity. No one can get a life sentence in federal prison for marijuana based solely on the amount involved.

A few states—including Mississippi, Montana, Nevada, Oklahoma, and Texas—do, in fact, allow judges to impose a life sentence even for a first pot offense. Texas applies this provision only to trafficking offenses and to possession cases involving a ton or more of marijuana, and in Nevada, a life sentence is possible with possession of 10,000 pounds—five tons—or more. In the other states mentioned above, a first-time marijuana offense can draw a life sentence only if the case involves the sale, manufacture, or cultivation of the drug, not mere possession.

The Claim:

"Even peaceful marijuana smokers sentenced to 'life MMS' [mandatory minimum sentences] must serve a life sentence with no chance of parole."

Look Again:

Mandatory minimums generally do not apply in cases involving only simple possession of marijuana, particularly for a first offense. Rather, states that set mandatory minimums for marijuana offenses usually apply them only to the cultivation, sale, or trafficking of the drug. So unless "peaceful marijuana smokers" are found guilty of more than simple possession, it is highly unlikely they will face a mandatory minimum sentence.

There are, however, a few very specific exceptions to this rule. In Louisiana, for instance, a first-time conviction for possession of marijuana on a school bus or within 1,000 feet of a school, religious building, or public housing triggers a mandatory minimum sentence of at least three months.

In the great majority of cases, people serving long prison terms for marijuana have been convicted of crimes far more serious than simple possession. They have previous felony convictions or have been found guilty of such offenses as distributing, selling, manufacturing, or illegally importing drugs, money-laundering, violating parole or drug kingpin statutes, or various combinations of those crimes.

It's also true that a number of inmates technically serving time for marijuana possession have been convicted of that offense *along with* another, more serious crime. Most often in cases like this, the sentence for marijuana possession is simply running concurrent with (at the same time as) the more serious sentence. So while they may indeed have been convicted for marijuana possession, it was the other, more serious crime that put them behind bars.

EVALUATING THE AUTHOR'S ARGUMENTS:

The author seems to take great care to list exceptions to his arguments, stating that some states do in fact require mandatory prison sentences for first-time marijuana offenders. For example, he states that Louisiana requires a minimum sentence of three months for a first-time conviction for possession on a school bus or within one thousand feet of a school. Does this strengthen or weaken his overall argument? Why or why not?

The War on Drugs Must Continue

"From the standpoint of protecting children, teens and the public health, reducing marijuana use makes eminent sense."

Joseph A. Califano Jr.

Although marijuana arrests are up 30 percent and marijuana use has waned over the last several years, the war against drugs is far from over. Recent studies show the number of young people in treatment for marijuana dependence is higher than ever, and the number of teen emergency room admissions for marijuana has spiked since 1999. According to the article "The Right Drug to Target," author Joseph A. Califano Jr. argues that public policy and law enforcement efforts should more effectively target marijuana use. Offenders should face stricter penalties and should attend classes on the dangers of marijuana.

AS YOU READ, CONSIDER THE FOLLOWING QUESTIONS:

1. If the author advocates harsher penalties for marijuana use, why is he not pleased about the 30 percent increase in marijuana arrests?
2. What punishment does the author suggest for kids arrested for marijuana possession?
3. What percentage of twelve- to seventeen-year-olds say they would be able to buy marijuana within a day?

Washington Post, May 17, 2005, p. A21 for "The Right Drug to Target: Cutting Marijuana Use Calls for More than Tough Policing," by Joseph A. Califano, Jr. Copyright © 2005 The Washington Post Company. Reproduced by permission of the author.

The increased potency of today's marijuana and the greater knowledge we have of the dangers of using marijuana justify the increased attention that law enforcement is giving to illegal possession of the drug. But the disappointing reality is that a nearly 30 percent increase in marijuana arrests does not translate into a comparable reduction in use of the drug. Something more is needed.

[Former New York City mayor] Rudolph Giuliani's success in slashing [the city's] crime rate by, among other things, going after low-level street crimes such as smoking and selling small amounts of marijuana inspired many other mayors to follow suit. When President [George W.] Bush announced in 2002 a goal of reducing illegal drug use by 10 percent in two years and 25 percent in five years, he knew he had to focus on cutting marijuana use. Eliminating all other illegal drug use combined would not even get him close to his highly touted objective.

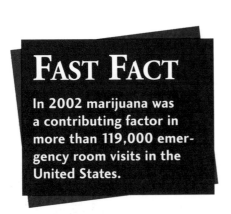

FAST FACT

In 2002 marijuana was a contributing factor in more than 119,000 emergency room visits in the United States.

The Need to Reduce Use

From the standpoint of protecting children, teens and the public health, reducing marijuana use makes eminent sense. For even though marijuana use has leveled off or waned slightly over the past several years, the number of children and teenagers in treatment for marijuana dependence and abuse has jumped 142 percent since 1992, and the number of teen emergency room admissions in which marijuana is implicated is up almost 50 percent since 1999. Though alcohol remains by far the teen substance of choice, teens are three times likelier to be in treatment for marijuana than for alcohol (and six times likelier to be in treatment for marijuana than for all other illegal drugs combined).

As has been true of tobacco since the 1960s, we've learned a lot about the dangers of marijuana since the 1970s. The drug adversely affects short-term memory, the ability to concentrate and motor skills.

Recent studies indicate that it increases the likelihood of depression, schizophrenia and other serious mental health problems. Nora Volkow, director of the National Institute on Drug Abuse, has repeatedly expressed concern about the adverse impact of marijuana on the brain, a matter of particular moment for youngsters whose brains are still in the development stage. Volkow has stated: "There is no question marijuana can be addictive; that argument is over. The most important thing right now is to understand the vulnerability of young, developing brains to these increased concentrations of cannabis."

Kids and Marijuana

The issue of marijuana use (and most illegal drug use) is all about kids. If we can get kids not to smoke marijuana before they reach age 21, they are virtually certain never to do so. So let's do more than trumpet the arrest rate. Let's focus on discouraging children and teens from getting involved with the drug in the first place.

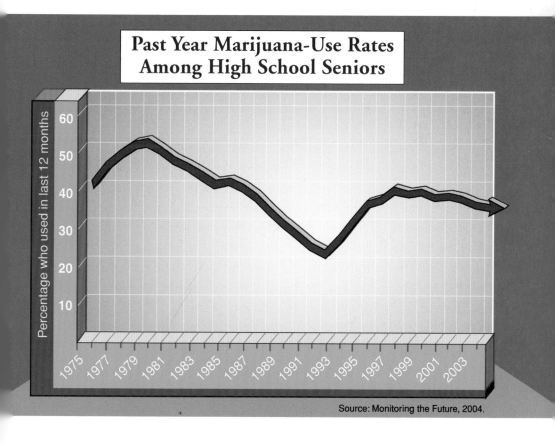

Source: Monitoring the Future, 2004.

Narcotics detectives in Brooklyn, New York, stand behind a table filled with seven hundred pounds of seized marijuana.

This begins with understanding the importance of preventing kids from becoming cigarette smokers. Most kids who smoke cigarettes will not smoke marijuana, but a 2003 survey of 12- to 17-year-olds, conducted by the National Center on Addiction and Substance Abuse (CASA) at Columbia University, reveals that teens who smoke cigarettes are much likelier than non-smokers to try marijuana; they are also likelier to become regular marijuana users.

The next question is how to make public policies, including law enforcement approaches, more effective in discouraging marijuana use. Availability is the mother of use, so doing a far better job of reducing availability is high on the list. Beyond that—and recognizing that reducing demand is key to that goal—we should use the increased arrest rate as an opportunity to discourage use.

Stiffer Punishments

Years ago, while I was visiting Los Angeles, then-Mayor Dick Riordan told me that in his city kids were arrested an average of nine times for possession of marijuana before anything happened to them. I have since discovered that this situation is common in many American communities. Most kids do not even get a slap on the wrist the first few times they're nabbed for smoking a joint. As a result, we let them sink deeper and deeper into drug use, with its dangers to their physical, mental and emotional development and its risk of addiction.

I am not suggesting that we put kids in jail for smoking pot. But why not treat a teen arrested for marijuana use much the same way we treat a teen arrested for drunk driving? Why not require kids arrested for marijuana possession to attend classes to learn about the dangers of marijuana use and to develop some skills (and the will) to decline the next time they are offered the drug? The incentive to attend such classes would be the threat of the alternative: for the first couple of arrests, loss of a driver's license or a fine stiff enough to hurt; for continued use, a few nights in a local prison. Getting kids to attend sessions designed to discourage their marijuana use would give some practical meaning to increased law enforcement and would bring reductions in drug use more in line with increased arrest rates.

More Help from Parents

These steps will help, but the fact is that we cannot arrest our way out of the teen marijuana problem when (in a recent CASA survey) 40 percent of 12- to 17-year-olds report that they can buy the drug within a day, and 21 percent say they can buy it within an hour.

Parents are the first line of defense. Parents must understand that the drug available today is far more potent than what they might have smoked in the 1970s. For their children, smoking marijuana is not a harmless rite of passage but rather a dangerous game of Russian roulette.

EVALUATING THE AUTHOR'S ARGUMENTS:

The author argues that the number of children and teens in treatment for marijuana dependence has jumped 142 percent since 1992. Do you find that statistic troubling? Can you think of any reasons for such a huge increase?

The War on Drugs Is a Failure

Angela French

"The White House Office of National Drug Control Policy (ONDCP)... has wasted $4.2 billion... on media advertising [and] fighting state legislation."

The so-called War on Drugs is an utter failure, according to Citizens Against Government Waste (CAGW.) The White House Office of National Drug Control Policy (ONDCP) has thrown billions of dollars of taxpayer money toward expensive antidrug programs—aimed mostly at marijuana—with zero results. Worse yet, after being bombarded with costly anti-marijuana media campaigns on a frequent basis, some teens believe that marijuana is a bigger danger than most hard drugs like cocaine and LSD. In her report *Up in Smoke: Office of National Drug Control Policy's Wasted Efforts on the War on Drugs*, Angela French outlines the dramatic failure of the government to reduce drug use among America's youth.

AS YOU READ, CONSIDER THE FOLLOWING QUESTIONS:
1. According to the author, instead of wasting money on propaganda-filled news videos, what should the government do to reduce drug use?
2. What was the purpose of the national youth Anti-Drug Media Campaign?

French, Angela. From *Through the Looking Glass: Up in Smoke: Office of National Drug Control Policy's Wasted Efforts on the War on Drugs*, Washington, DC: Citizens Against Government Waste, May 11, 2005. Copyright © CITIZENS AGAINST GOVERNMENT WASTE. Reproduced by permission.

3. According to the author, what is the hidden agenda of the Anti-Drug Media Campaign?

Established in 1988 to oversee all aspects of America's war on drugs and to coordinate U.S. domestic and international anti-drug efforts, the White House Office of National Drug Control Policy (ONDCP) has morphed into a federal wasteland, throwing taxpayer money toward numerous high-priced drug control programs that have failed to show results. After 17 years of operation and funding, ONDCP has not achieved its objectives of reducing "illicit drug use, manufacturing, and trafficking, drug-related crime and violence, and drug-related health consequences."

Allocation of Drug Control Spending to Marijuana Versus Other Drugs, 2004, in Billions

Function	Total Anti-Drug Spending	Marijuana Percentage	Marijuana Spending
Prohibition Total	**$6,846.8**	**20.9%**	**$1,431.0**
Intelligence	$465.2	20.9%	$97.2
Interdiction	$2,534.2	20.9%	$529.6
International	$1,159.3	20.9%	$242.3
Investigation	$2,214.5	20.9%	$462.8
Prosecution	$112.9	20.9%	$23.6
State and Local Assistance	$360.7	20.9%	$75.4
Prevention	**$1,543.5**	**72.1%**	**$1,112.9**
Research & Development	**$1,056.1**	**72.1%**	**$761.4**
Treatment	**$2,421.2**	**15.1%**	**$365.6**
Grand Total	**$11,867.4**		**$3,670.9**

Source: Federal Marijuana Policy: A Preliminary Assessment, June 2005.

Instead of curbing America's drug problem, ONDCP has wasted $4.2 billion since fiscal 1997 on media advertising, fighting state legislation, and deficient anti-drug trafficking programs. ONDCP's fiscal 2005 budget of $507 million will fund such diverse functions as local law enforcement, cracking down on medical marijuana use, drug research and treatment, and the eradication of coca crops in Latin America.

Many of ONDCP's outreach efforts focus on reducing marijuana use. In fact, since Arizona and California passed medicinal marijuana laws in November 1996, ONDCP has been intent on reducing the popularity of marijuana in the U.S. The agency created the National Youth Anti-Drug Media Campaign in 1998 just for that purpose. ONDCP also began campaigning against state ballot initiatives legalizing the use of medicinal marijuana, which is an infringement upon states' rights, a blatant misuse of tax dollars, and in contravention of ONDCP's original mission. The White House's drug office should use its resources to root out major drug operations in the U.S. instead of creating propaganda-filled news videos and flying across the country on the taxpayers' dime. . . .

The National Youth Anti-Drug Media Campaign

One of ONDCP's cornerstone programs, the National Youth Anti-Drug Media Campaign, has been an utter failure. The five-year effort has wasted $2 billion on propaganda with no measurable results. The project was initially created "to educate and enable youth to reject illegal drugs, especially marijuana and inhalants," but has been unsuccessful in reducing drug use amongst America's youth. In addition to its chronic failure, a January 2005 Government Accountability Office (GAO) report found the advertising campaign violated federal advertising laws.

The media campaign was the pet project of former ONDCP Director ("drug czar") Gen. Barry R. McCaffrey. In November 1996, just nine days after Arizona and California voted in favor of their new medicinal marijuana initiatives, the White House drug czar called the first meeting at his office to mobilize "his troops to combat the spread of what he had previously called 'Cheech & Chong' medicine." [Cheech Marin and Tommy Chong were a comedy duo who found a wide audience in the 1970s and 1980s for their stand-up routines, which were based on the era's hippie, free love, and especially drug culture movements.] McCaffrey gathered 40 federal and private sector "drug warriors" to brainstorm over how to increase efforts on the war on drugs. The outcome was the National Youth Anti-Drug Media Campaign, which was touted as an educational outreach effort, but remains nothing more than a thinly-veiled propaganda scheme focused on curtailing further medicinal marijuana initiatives on state ballots.

FAST FACT

The federal government spends more than $4 billion a year on marijuana-related activities.

Critics immediately began questioning whether the federal government should be involved in state ballot measures at all. The head of the Partnership for Responsible Drug Information, Thomas H. Haines, stated that "The use of government resources to politic on controversial issues is clearly against ethics, as well as the law stating that federal employees can not take public positions for or against legislation under consideration.". . .

The Failure of Anti-Marijuana Ads

In another attempt to reduce drug use, ONDCP creates anti-drug clips, fact sheets and newsletters on its website. The ads are created to specifically reach the targeted audience. A majority of the clips focus on keeping kids away from marijuana, and encourage parents to enforce that initiative. Of the 26 youth-targeted television ads available on ONDCP's website, 17 of them, or 65 percent, specifically mention pot; only 2 ads mention another type of illicit drug. Of the 65 anti-drug print ads available, 34, or 52 percent, specifically stress not using marijuana. In one television youth ad, "Jose" pays tribute to a classmate who opened his eyes to poetry and education, but the classmate was caught with a "nickelbag of herb" leading to expulsion from high school and failure in life. In another television ad, a teenager finds out she was pregnant after making a wrong decision because

U.S. Customs Service inspectors search a car that alleged smugglers had loaded with over eighty pounds of marijuana at the U.S.-Mexico border in San Diego.

of marijuana. This commercial ran during the 2005 Super Bowl, where $2.4 million bought a 30-second slot.

Despite all the funding for the commercials, the television shows and Internet clips, the National Youth Anti-Drug Media Campaign has failed to achieve its overall goal of reducing youth drug use. In September 1998, the National Institute on Drug Abuse (NIDA) competitively awarded a grant to Westat, Inc., a health survey research company, to conduct a "science-based evaluation" of the program. Every Westat report has concluded that there have been no significant changes among America's young people that can be solely attributed to ONDCP's expensive anti-drug campaign.

In its December 22, 2003 ONDCP report, Westat reported on the Marijuana Initiative, which ONDCP began as part of the media campaign in 2002. According to the evaluation, "[t]here is little evidence of direct favorable Campaign effects on youth, either for the Marijuana Initiative period or for the Campaign as [a] whole . . . youth who were more exposed to Campaign messages are no more likely to hold favorable beliefs or intentions about marijuana than are youth less exposed to those messages, both during the Marijuana Initiative period and over the entire course of the Campaign."

Westat also reported that "[t]he previous two reports in this series . . . suggested that the Campaign was not achieving its major objective of affecting youth marijuana use, and even showed some evidence of an unfavorable delayed effect of the Campaign on youth." The report also showed that from 2000 to 2003, the percentage of America's youth definitely not intending to try marijuana was reduced by a scant .6 percent, from 87.5 percent in 2000 to 86.9 percent in 2003. Clearly, the money spent on television, print, radio and Internet ads was not helping ONDCP to achieve its goal.

The Wrong Message

Despite the large amount of taxpayer money invested in educating teens about the harmful effects of drug use, the trends of disapproval of drug use among high school seniors remained relatively consistent during the period of the media campaign. According to the federally-funded "Monitoring the Future" study, since 1998, there has been a modest decline in use of drugs by teenagers. ONDCP's ads heavily emphasized marijuana, but the use of many drugs mentioned little or not at all in the media campaign, including alcohol, are down by roughly the same amount.

Although the percentage of teenagers using marijuana is down, the 2004 results show a slight increase of 8th, 10th, and 12th graders using hard drugs, including inhalants, cocaine and heroin. Also, according to the latest survey, more 8th graders see a greater risk in smoking marijuana occasionally than in taking LSD regularly, taking ecstasy occasionally, trying crack cocaine, or drinking nearly every day. Since 1998, more and more 8th graders believe any marijuana use is a great risk, yet fewer 8th graders believe there is great risk in using inhalants or LSD regularly, suggesting that the campaign may actually be steering kids toward the most dangerous drugs.

EVALUATING THE AUTHOR'S ARGUMENTS:

The author writes that in 2004 there was a slight increase of eighth, tenth, and twelfth graders using hard drugs, including cocaine and heroin. Do you think this had something to do with the fact that most anti-drug messaging was focused on marijuana? Why or why not?

Marijuana Should Be Decriminalized, Not Legalized

James Austin

Most policy makers in favor of decriminalizing marijuana focus on the huge decrease in government expenditures for the arrest, prosecution, and imprisonment of marijuana offenders. However, this argument fails to address the fact that most government expenditures are fixed, and a reduction in marijuana arrests would not necessarily yield any sort of savings. The real benefit of marijuana decriminalization, according to author James Austin in his report, *Rethinking the Consequences of Decriminalizing Marijuana,* is the ability of the criminal justice system to reallocate its resources to more serious crimes and public safety issues. This report was published by NORML, the National Organization for the Reform of Marijuana Laws.

"The major benefit of decriminalization . . . would be the ability of the criminal justice system to focus on more important public safety activities."

AS YOU READ, CONSIDER THE FOLLOWING QUESTIONS:

1. What is wrong with past studies measuring the effects of decriminalizing marijuana, according to Austin?

Austin, James. *Rethinking the Consequences of Decriminalizing Marijuana,* Washington, DC: NORML, 2005. Copyright © 2005 NORML. Reproduced by permission.

2. What does the author claim is the real benefit of decriminalizing marijuana?
3. According to the author, what was the effect of California's marijuana legislation in the 1970s?

The past three decades have witnessed a stormy and controversial debate about the possible merits to society that might be brought about by decriminalizing or legalizing marijuana. Beginning in 1973 with Oregon, 12 states (Alaska, California, Colorado, Maine, Minnesota, Mississippi, New York, Nebraska, Nevada, North Carolina, Ohio, and Oregon) have in some manner altered their existing laws to reduce the penalties for marijuana possession.

A number of local cities have also modified their local ordinances and criminal justice practices to decriminalize pot (Berkeley, Oakland and San Francisco, California; Breckenridge, Colorado; Amherst, Massachusetts; Madison and Milwaukee, Wisconsin; Urbana and Carbondale, Illinois; and Columbia, Missouri; among others).

Arguments for Decriminalization

There are three central arguments supportive of the decriminalization movement which have been advanced in these and other jurisdictions. Perhaps the most powerful and appealing argument for marijuana decriminalization (and/or decriminalizing other drugs) is that it would save a huge amount of government money now being spent on the enforcement of such laws. The basic tenets of the cost saving argument can be summarized as follows:

- The criminal justice system, ranging from police to corrections, now allocates a significant portion of its budgets arresting, prosecuting, sentencing and incarcerating marijuana users, dealers and others involved in the illegal drug infrastructure (e.g., transporters, manufacturers of drug paraphernalia, etc.).
- If these behaviors would no longer be labeled as criminal, criminal justice agencies would reduce the enforcement and processing tasks now associated with such crimes.

- There is a direct relationship between the proportion of arrests or cases processed for marijuana crimes by the criminal justice system and the amount of money expended by these same agencies.
- By reducing or eliminating these marijuana related events, there would be a proportionate decrease in the agency expenses.

This perspective has led to some fairly substantial claims regarding the amount of money to be saved by taxpayers if marijuana were decriminalized. For example, a recent study by Scott Bates (2004) claimed that Alaska was spending $25–30 million per year enforcing marijuana prohibition laws. Further, since there is no link between marijuana use and criminal behavior, there would be no impact on crime. And, if the purchase of marijuana were to be taxed as a legal commodity, tax revenues would increase by about $10–20 million per year. So, voters were promised that a net swing of $35–$50 million per year would appear in the state's coffers if marijuana were decriminalized.

FAST FACT

Of all drug arrests, 46 percent are for marijuana.

Jeffrey A. Miron from MIT made a similar claim in his assessment of drug laws in Massachusetts. Applying the same assumptions used by Bates, he estimated that the state would reduce its criminal justice expenditures by $120.6 million per year. The largest savings would be in the courts ($68.5 million), followed by police ($40.3 million) and corrections ($13.6 million). And, Michael Aldrich, Tod Mikuriya, and Gordon Bronwell have claimed that California's pioneering decriminalization law (SB 95) was generating over $30 million per year in reduced police costs. . . .

The Problem with Past Studies

The primary problem with these estimates is that while they accurately reflect the proportionate level of costs they are not useful in estimating the savings to be realized if marijuana sales and possession were no longer criminalized. In fact, this somewhat simplistic and static cost benefit model generates highly misleading and exaggerated cost savings claims because it fails to recognize that government agency budgets are relatively fixed and operate independent of the level of activities or events (arrests, prosecutions, and sentencing) reported by the agency.

Indeed, decriminalization will have only a marginal impact on criminal justice costs. This is not to say that decriminalization would have a trivial effect on costs or that it should not be aggressively pursued by state and federal policy makers. The major benefit of decriminalization, in addition to eliminating the needless arrest, prosecution, and court disposition of over 700,000 people each year, would be the ability of the criminal justice system to focus on more important public safety activities. . . .

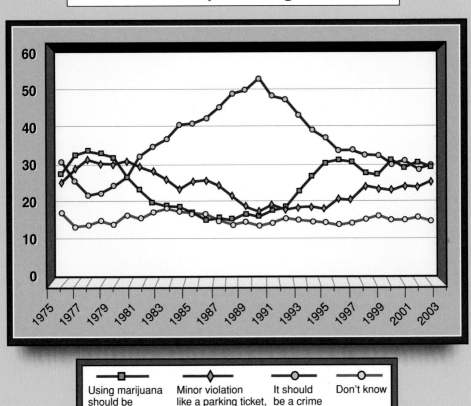

Attitudes of High School Seniors Toward Marijuana Legalization

Legend:
- Using marijuana should be entirely legal
- Minor violation like a parking ticket, not a crime
- It should be a crime
- Don't know

Source: NSDHU, National Survey on Drug Use and Health, 2003.

Marijuana's Impact on Arrests and Court Processing

Despite the large swell of legislative activity at both the state and local level, the number of persons arrested for marijuana possession and sale has grown significantly. In 1970 there was an estimated 188,682 arrests for the drug—by 2003 the number had increased to 755,000. So it's clear that despite the decriminalization effort, the chances of a marijuana user being arrested have significantly increased.

Although a large and increasing number of persons are arrested each year for marijuana violations, as a proportion of total number of criminal justice arrest and felony court convictions, marijuana cases are relatively low percentages of police and court's workload. . . .

Eliminating the marijuana arrest pool would have only a marginal effect on the universe of arrests and the workload of the police.

The same can be said about the impact on the courts. There are an estimated one million felony convictions by state and federal courts. Of this number only 69,500 convictions were for marijuana violations of which 44,200 are possession convictions. . . .

The Real Benefit of Decriminalization

Given the large amount of discretion enjoyed by police and the courts in terms of how resources are deployed, it is quite possible that as the emphasis on one crime is reduced, resources are re-directed to other crimes. Indeed, this is one of the major justifications for decriminalization of marijuana—not so much that it would reduce criminal justice costs. Rather it would allow the criminal justice system to focus on more serious crimes.

To better understand this phenomenon, one needs to examine the example of California's decriminalization reforms in the 1970s. California on two occasions in the 1970s enacted major legislative changes designed to lessen the reach of the criminal justice system on marijuana use. In 1972, then Senator George Deukmejian successfully sponsored legislation that allowed persons charged with minor drug offenses and other misdemeanor crimes to be diverted from future criminal prosecution if they agreed to participate and complete a pretrial diversion program. In 1975, the California legislature enacted Senate Bill 95 which took effect on January 1, 1976 and had the following provisions:

A state trooper cuts down marijuana plants.

1. No arrest or booking for individuals apprehended in possession of small amounts of marijuana;
2. No jail or incarceration for persons convicted of possession of small amounts of marijuana;
3. Furnishing of small amount of marijuana for no consideration is treated as simple possession, not sale;
4. Transportation of small amounts of marijuana is treated as simple possession, not felony transportation;

5. Elimination of life-long criminal records for marijuana posession arrests and convictions, and placing a two-year limit on the retention of such records and the use of such records against individuals arrested and convicted of specified offenses;

6. Abolition of recidivist penalties for simple possession, giving away and transporting small amounts of marijuana.

Many observers have concluded that the California legislation has been very successful in terms of reducing arrests and saving large amounts of money. [One study] found that after S.B. 95 took effect, the number of marijuana arrests declined from a pre 1976 rate of approximately 100,000 per year to about 25,000 per year. Using a proportionate costs benefit model, the authors concluded that criminal justice expenditures declined by 24 percent from 1974 to 1984 with a [cumulative] savings of $360 million. They conclude that: "It is rare that a single legal change has such an immediate and drastic effect on arrests and enforcement costs in a state."

EVALUATING THE AUTHOR'S ARGUMENTS:

In this report the author refutes several past studies measuring the effectiveness of marijuana decriminalization. Do you think this makes his overall argument weaker or stronger?

Marijuana Should Be Legalized, Not Decriminalized

Norm Stamper

"It's time to accept drug use as a right of adult Americans."

All drugs should be legalized, argues Norm Stamper, a former police chief. Not just pot but also heroin, cocaine, meth, psychotropics, hallucinogenic mushrooms, and LSD. Responsible drug use should be a civil liberty—and a right of adult Americans. By enabling private companies to cultivate and package the drugs, enforcing standards of sanitation and potency, the government could police the industry much as it does the alcohol industry today. The results would reduce prison overcrowding and would lead to a huge reduction in street crime, ultimately making America a better place to live and raise a family. Stamper argues these points in his opinion piece for the *Los Angeles Times*, published in 2005.

AS YOU READ, CONSIDER THE FOLLOWING QUESTIONS:
1. What does Stamper say are some of the problems law enforcement faces with illegal drug use and peddling?

Stamper, Norm. From "Let Those Dopers Be," in *Los Angeles Times*, Op-ed, October 16, 2005, M1. Reproduced by permission of the author.

2. How would "regulated legalization" work, according to Stamper?
3. According to the author, drug abuse is not a criminal matter. What does he call it?

Sometimes people in law enforcement will hear it whispered that I'm a former cop who favors decriminalization of marijuana laws, and they'll approach me the way they might a traitor or snitch. So let me set the record straight.

Yes, I was a cop for 34 years, the last six of which I spent as chief of Seattle's police department. But no, I don't favor decriminalization. I favor legalization, and not just of pot but of all drugs, including heroin, cocaine, meth, psychotropics, mushrooms and LSD.

Decriminalization, as my colleagues in the drug reform movement hasten to inform me, takes the crime out of using drugs but continues to classify possession and use as a public offense, punishable by fines.

Estimated Numbers (in Thousands) and Percentages of Daily Marijuana Users, by Age and Gender: 2003

Daily Marijuana Users		
Characteristic	Percent	Number
Age (Years)		
12 to 17	1.1	282
18 to 25	4.3	1,375
26 or older	0.8	1,433
Gender		
Male	2.0	2,253
Female	0.7	837
Total	**1.3**	**3,090**

Source: National Survey on Drug Use and Health, 2003.

I've never understood why adults shouldn't enjoy the same right to use *verboten* drugs as they have to suck on a Marlboro or knock back a scotch and water.

Effects of Drug and Alcohol Regulation

Prohibition of alcohol fell flat on its face. The prohibition of other drugs rests on an equally wobbly foundation. Not until we choose to frame responsible drug use—not an oxymoron in my dictionary—as a civil liberty will we be able to recognize the abuse of drugs, including alcohol, for what it is: a medical, not a criminal, matter.

As a cop, I bore witness to the multiple lunacies of the "war on drugs." Lasting far longer than any other of our national conflicts, the drug war has been prosecuted with equal vigor by Republican and Democratic administrations, with one president after another—Nixon, Ford, Carter, Reagan, Bush, Clinton, Bush—delivering sanctimonious sermons, squandering vast sums of taxpayer money and cheerleading law enforcers from the safety of the sidelines.

It's not a stretch to conclude that our draconian approach to drug use is the most injurious domestic policy since slavery. Want to cut back on prison overcrowding and save a bundle on the construction of new facilities? Open the doors, let the nonviolent drug offenders go.

The huge increases in federal and state prison populations during the 1980s and '90s (from 139 per 100,000 residents in 1980 to 482 per 100,000 in 2003) were mainly for drug convictions. In 1980, 580,900 Americans were arrested on drug charges. By 2003, that figure had ballooned to 1,678,200. We're making more arrests for drug offenses than for murder, manslaughter, forcible rape and aggravated assault combined. Feel safer?

Effects of Drug Regulation on Law Enforcement

I've witnessed the devastating effects of open-air drug markets in residential neighborhoods: children recruited as runners, mules and lookouts; drug dealers and innocent citizens shot dead in firefights between rival traffickers bent on protecting or expanding their markets; dedicated narcotics officers tortured and killed in the line of duty; prisons filled with nonviolent drug offenders; and drug-related foreign policies that foster political instability, wreak health and environmental disasters, and make life even tougher for indigenous subsistence farmers in places such as Latin America and Afghanistan. All because we like our drugs—and can't have them without breaking the law.

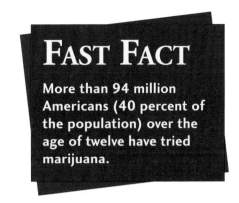

FAST FACT

More than 94 million Americans (40 percent of the population) over the age of twelve have tried marijuana.

As an illicit commodity, drugs cost and generate extravagant sums of (laundered, untaxed) money, a powerful magnet for character-challenged police officers. Although small in numbers of offenders, there isn't a major police force—the Los Angeles Police Department included—that has escaped the problem: cops, sworn to uphold the law, seizing and converting drugs to their own use, planting dope on suspects, robbing and extorting pushers, taking up dealing themselves, intimidating or murdering witnesses.

In declaring a war on drugs, we've declared war on our fellow citizens. War requires "hostiles"—enemies we can demonize, fear and loathe. This unfortunate categorization of millions of our citizens justifies treating them as dope fiends, evil-doers, less than human. That grants political license to ban the exchange or purchase of clean needles or to withhold methadone from heroin addicts motivated to kick the addiction.

President [George W.] Bush has even said no to medical marijuana. Why would he want to "coddle" the enemy? Even if the enemy is a suffering AIDS or cancer patient for whom marijuana promises palliative, if not therapeutic, powers.

As a nation, we're long overdue for a soul-searching, coldly analytical look at both the "drug scene" and the drug war. Such candor would reveal the futility of our current policies, exposing the embarrassingly meager return on our massive enforcement investment (about $69 billion a year, according to Jack Cole, founder and executive director of Law Enforcement Against Prohibition).

How Legalization Would Work

How would "regulated legalization" work? It would:

1. Permit private companies to compete for licenses to cultivate, harvest, manufacture, package and peddle drugs.

2. Create a new federal regulatory agency (with no apologies to libertarians or paleo-conservatives).
3. Set and enforce standards of sanitation, potency and purity.
4. Ban advertising.
5. Impose (with congressional approval) taxes, fees and fines to be used for drug-abuse prevention and treatment and to cover the costs of administering the new regulatory agency.
6. Police the industry much as alcoholic beverage control agencies keep a watch on bars and liquor stores at the state level.

Teenagers attend the 2003 Seattle Hempfest, a weekend festival aimed at changing the nation's marijuana laws.

Such reforms would in no way excuse drug users who commit crimes: driving while impaired, providing drugs to minors, stealing an iPod or a Lexus, assaulting one's spouse, abusing one's child. The message is simple. Get loaded, commit a crime, do the time. These reforms would yield major reductions in a host of predatory street crimes, a disproportionate number of which are committed by users who resort to stealing in order to support their habit or addiction.

Regulated legalization would soon dry up most stockpiles of currently illicit drugs—substances of uneven, often questionable quality (including "bunk," i.e., fakes such as oregano, gypsum, baking powder or even poisons passed off as the genuine article). It would extract from today's drug dealing the obscene profits that attract the needy and the greedy and fuel armed violence. And it would put most of those certifiably frightening crystal meth labs out of business once and for all.

Other Benefits to Drug Legalization

Combined with treatment, education and other public health programs for drug abusers, regulated legalization would make your city or town an infinitely healthier place to live and raise a family. It would make being a cop a much safer occupation, and it would lead to greater police accountability and improved morale and job satisfaction.

But wouldn't regulated legalization lead to more users and, more to the point, drug abusers? Probably, though no one knows for sure—our leaders are too timid even to broach the subject in polite circles, much less to experiment with new policy models. My own prediction? We'd see modest increases in use, negligible increases in abuse.

The demand for illicit drugs is as strong as the nation's thirst for bootleg booze during Prohibition. It's a demand that simply will not dwindle or dry up. Whether to find God, heighten sexual arousal, relieve physical pain, drown one's sorrows or simply feel good, for millennia people have turned to mood- and mind-altering substances.

They're not about to stop, no matter what their government says or does. It's time to accept drug use as a right of adult Americans, treat drug abuse as a public health problem and end the madness of an unwinnable war.

EVALUATING THE AUTHOR'S ARGUMENTS:

As mentioned in the article, the author is the former chief of the Seattle police department. Do you find it ironic that he would favor outright legalization of all drugs? Does his experience make him more or less qualified to make these arguments?

Facts About Marijuana

Editor's note: These facts can be used in reports or papers to reinforce or add credibility when making important points or claims.

General Information
- Marijuana is a mixture of flowers, stems, seeds, and leaves of the hemp plant *Cannabis sativa.* Although it contains hundreds of chemicals, the active ingredient is THC.
- Marijuana can be smoked or mixed with food and drink.
- Medical marijuana advocates claim that it helps alleviate symptoms related to cancer, AIDS, glaucoma, Alzheimer's, multiple sclerosis, and more.

Marijuana in the World
- Marijuana is the most commonly used illicit drug in the world.
- Medical marijuana is legal in Canada.
- Marijuana has been decriminalized in a number of countries, including the Netherlands, Spain, Italy, Portugal, Belgium, Germany, Croatia, Switzerland, and Great Britain.

Marijuana and the United States
- About 94.8 million Americans aged twelve and older have tried marijuana at least once during their lifetimes.
- About 3.2 million Americans report using marijuana on a daily basis.
- In the United States marijuana is illegal under federal law, but twelve states have legalized medical marijuana.
- According to a 2005 Gallup poll, about one-third of Americans believe that marijuana should be legal.
- According to the same poll, 78 percent of Americans believe that medical marijuana should be legal.

- Marijuana is considered a Schedule I drug, which means that the government has decided it has a high potential for abuse and no currently accepted medical use.
- Marinol is a synthetic form of THC that is legally prescribed in the United States.
- According to policy analyst Paul Armentano, Marinol costs patients two hundred to eight hundred dollars a month.
- In a 2005 poll an estimated 115,000 people have obtained marijuana recommendations from doctors in the United States.
- Marijuana arrests have increased 113 percent since 1990.
- In a 2005 report the Sentencing Project found that almost half of the yearly 1.5 million drug arrests in the United States were for marijuana.
- According to the Office of National Drug Control Policy, only a small percentage of people sentenced in federal court for marijuana offenses were for simple possession; the majority were convicted of trafficking.
- In 2003 the government spent $3.3 billion on the prevention and treatment of marijuana.
- Critics disagree on whether or not marijuana is dangerous; in 2004 it was involved in more than two hundred thousand emergency room visits, but no one has ever died from a marijuana overdose.
- According to the DEA, one marijuana cigarette deposits approximately four times more tar in the lungs than a filtered tobacco cigarette.
- Of adults who had been arrested for serious offenses in 2004, almost half had used marijuana in the past year, according to the Substance Abuse and Mental Health Services Administration.
- Americans spend about $10.4 billion a year on marijuana, according to the DEA.
- Only 58 percent of twelfth graders said that smoking marijuana regularly is a "great risk," according to a 2005 survey.

Americans for Safe Access (ASA)
1322 Webster St., Suite 208
Oakland, CA 94612
(888) 929-4367
e-mail: info@safeaccessnow.org
Web site: www.safeaccessnow.org

Americans for Safe Access works to protect the rights of patients and doctors to use marijuana for medical purposes. ASA's mission is to ensure safe, legal access to marijuana for all who are helped by it. The organization provides legal training for lawyers and patients, medical information for doctors and patients, media support for court cases, and activist training to organizers.

Common Sense for Drug Policy (CSDP)
1377-C Spencer Ave.
Lancaster, PA 17603
(717) 299-0600
fax: (717) 393-4953
e-mail: info@csdp.org
Web site: www.csdp.org

CSDP is a nonprofit organization dedicated to reforming drug policy. The organization disseminates factual information and comments on existing laws, policies, and practices. CSDP advocates the regulation and control of marijuana in a manner similar to alcohol and subject to local, rather than federal, decisions.

Drug Enforcement Administration (DEA)
2401 Jefferson Davis Hwy., Suite 300
Alexandria, VA 22301
(800) 882-9539
Web site: www.dea.gov

The mission of the Drug Enforcement Administration is to enforce the controlled substances laws and regulations of the United States. It coordinates the activities of federal, state, and local agencies, and works with foreign governments to reduce the availability of illicit drugs in the United States.

Drug Free America Foundation
2600 9th St. N., Suite 200
St. Petersburg, FL 33704
(727) 828-0211
fax: (727) 828-0212
Web site: www.dfaf.org

Drug Free America Foundation is a drug prevention and policy organization committed to developing, promoting, and sustaining global strategies, policies, and laws that will reduce illegal drug use, drug addiction, and drug-related injury and death. The organization believes that the legalization of marijuana would be harmful to society.

Drug Policy Alliance
925 15th St. NW, 2nd Floor
Washington, DC 20005
(202) 216-0035
fax: (202) 216-0803
e-mail: dc@drugpolicy.org
Web site: www.drugpolicy.org

The Drug Policy Alliance believes in the sovereignty of individuals over their minds and bodies. Its position is that people should be punished for crimes committed against others, but not for using marijuana or other drugs as a personal choice. It promotes alternatives to the war on drugs in the United States and works to reduce the harms of drug misuse.

Drug Reform Coordination Network
1623 Connecticut Ave. NW, 3rd Floor
Washington, DC 20009
(202) 293-8340
fax: (202) 293-8344
e-mail: drcnet@drcnet.org
Web site: http://stopthedrugwar.org

The Drug Reform Coordination Network is an organization of educators, students, lawyers, health care professionals, academics, and others working to reform current drug policies. The organization believes that the federal government should reschedule marijuana to permit medical use.

Marijuana Policy Project (MPP)
PO Box 77492, Capitol Hill
Washington, DC 20013
e-mail: info@mpp.org
Web site: www.mpp.org

The Marijuana Policy Project is the largest marijuana policy reform organization in the United States. MPP works to minimize the harm associated with marijuana—both the consumption of marijuana and the laws that are intended to prohibit such use. The organization believes that the greatest harm associated with marijuana is prison, and focuses on removing criminal penalties for marijuana use. It also works to make marijuana medically available to seriously ill people who have the approval of their doctors.

The National Center on Addiction and Substance Abuse (CASA)
633 Third Ave., 19th Floor
New York, NY 10017-6706
(212) 841-5200
Web site: www.casacolumbia.org

The National Center on Addiction and Substance Abuse (CASA) at Columbia University is the only national organization that brings together under one roof all the professional disciplines needed to study and combat abuse of all substances—alcohol, nicotine, illegal drugs, prescription drugs, performance enhancing drugs—in all sectors of society.

National Institute on Drug Abuse (NIDA)
6001 Executive Blvd., Room 5213
Bethesda, MD 20892
(301) 443-1124
e-mail: information@nida.nih.gov
Web site: www.nida.nih.gov

The National Institute on Drug Abuse is one of the National Institutes of Health, a component of the U.S. Department of Health and Human Services. It supports scientific research on drug abuse and addiction. NIDA also works to disseminate the results of this research to policy makers, drug abuse practitioners, other health care practitioners, and the general public.

National Organization for the Reform of Marijuana Laws (NORML)
1600 K St. NW, Suite 501
Washington, DC 20006
(202) 483-5500
fax: (202) 483-0057
e-mail: norml@norml.org
Web site: www.norml.org

NORML is a public-interest advocacy group that opposes marijuana prohibition. The organization supports the right of adults to use marijuana responsibly for both personal and medical purposes. It believes that all penalties should be eliminated for responsible use. Further, NORML believes that a legally regulated market should be established where consumers can buy marijuana in a safe and secure environment.

Office of National Drug Control Policy (ONDCP)
PO Box 6000
Rockville, MD 20849-6000
(800) 666-3332
fax: (301) 519-5212
Web site: www.whitehousedrugpolicy.gov

The White House Office of National Drug Control Policy was established by the Anti–Drug Abuse Act of 1988. Its purpose is to establish policies, priorities, and objectives for the nation's drug control program. The goals of the program are to reduce illicit drug use, manufacturing, and trafficking; drug-related crime and violence; and drug-related health consequences.

RAND Drug Policy Research Center
PO Box 2138
Santa Monica, CA 90407-2138

(310) 393-0411
fax: (310) 393-4818
e-mail: dprc@rand.org
Web site: www.rand.org

The RAND Corporation is a research institution that seeks to improve public policy through research and analysis. RAND's Drug Policy Research Center disseminates information on the costs, prevention, and treatment of alcohol and drug abuse as well as on trends in drug-law enforcement.

The Substance Abuse and Mental Health Services Administration (SAMHSA)
1 Choke Cherry Rd.
Rockville, MD 20857
(240) 276-2000
fax: (240) 276-2010
Website: www.samhsa.gov

The Substance Abuse and Mental Health Services Administration (SAMHSA) has established a clear vision for its work—a life in the community for everyone. To realize this vision, the agency has sharply focused its mission on building resilience and facilitating recovery for people with or at risk for mental or substance use disorders. SAMHSA is gearing all of its resources—programs, policies, and grants—toward that outcome.

For Further Reading

Books

Booth, Martin. *Cannabis: A History*. New York: St. Martin's, 2004. In this comprehensive study, Booth examines the case for the decriminalization of marijuana and why it remains one of the country's hottest topics.

Brownlee, Nick. *The Complete Illustrated Guide to Cannabis*. London: Sanctuary, 2003. Brownlee explores a diverse range of views, from its medical merits to addictive qualities to deliver an honest, contemporary picture of marijuana.

Deitch, Robert. *Hemp—American History Revisited: The Plant with a Divided History*. New York: Algora, 2003. This colorful socioeconomic history clears the smoke obscuring hemp's role in battles between Colonial America and England, the Confederacy and the Union, and the marijuana lobby and its foes.

Esherick, Joan. *Dying for Acceptance: A Teen's Guide to Drug- and Alcohol-Related Health Issues*. Philadelphia: Mason Crest, 2005. Esherick explores the difficult choices teenagers face when it comes to drugs and alcohol, offering the knowledge they need to choose a lifestyle that is best for their own individual needs.

Gerber, Rudolph J. *Legalizing Marijuana: Drug Reform Policy and Prohibition Politics*. Westport, CT: Praeger, 2004. Gerber, a judge, presents the case in favor of marijuana legalization, at least for medical use, citing a host of research studies, which he claims have been ignored for decades.

Gottfried, Ted. *The Facts About Marijuana*. New York: Benchmark, 2005. Gottfried examines the facts about marijuana as a substance, along with the effects of marijuana on health, society, and politics.

Guy, Geoffrey, Brian A. Whittle, and Philip J. Robson, eds. *The Medicinal Use of Cannabis and Cannabinoids*. Chicago: Pharmaceutical, 2004. This book presents evidence of past, present, and even future medical utilizations of both cannabis and the herb's primary active constituents, the cannabinoids.

Huggins, Laura E., ed. *Drug War Deadlock: The Policy Battle Continues.* Stanford, CA: Hoover Institution, 2005. Huggins presents a diverse collection of readings from scholarly journals, government reports, think tank studies, newspapers, and books that offer a comprehensive look at the drug debate.

Marez, Curtis. *Drug Wars: The Political Economy of Narcotics.* Minneapolis: University of Minnesota Press, 2004. Marez, a cultural critic, examines two hundred years of writings, graphic works, films, and music that both demonize and celebrate the commerce in cocaine, marijuana, and opium.

Singer, Merrill. *Something Dangerous: Emergent and Changing Illicit Drug Use and Community Health.* Long Grove, IL: Waveland, 2006. The author assesses the role of youth in new drug use practices, the impact of illicit drug distribution and the war on drugs, and the public health risks of new trends in drug use behavior.

Steinberg, Michael K., Joseph J. Hobbs, and Kent Mathewson, eds. *Dangerous Harvest: Drug Plants and the Transformation of Indigenous Landscapes.* Oxford, UK: Oxford University Press, 2004. The purpose of this book is to explore this issue from a variety of perspectives, ranging from opium production in Afghanistan and Pakistan to peyote gardens in south Texas.

Periodicals

Clark, Ross. "Reefer Madness: Cannabis Is Not Harmless, Says Ross Clark, and Libertarians Are Wrong to Call for Its Legalisation," *Spectator,* January 28, 2006.

Cole, Sherwood O. "An Update on the Effects of Marijuana and Its Potential Medical Use: Forensic Focus," *Forensic Examiner,* Fall 2005.

Conant, Marcus. "Guest Editorial: Medical Marijuana," *Family Practice News,* July 1, 2005.

Cook, Margaret. "Cannabis: A Bad Trip for the Young," *New Statesman,* January 1, 2005.

Economist, "Reefer Madness," April 2, 2006.

Eggen, Dan. "Marijuana Becomes Focus of Drug War," *Washington Post*, May, 2005.

Greenberg, Gary. "Respectable Reefer," *Mother Jones*, November/December 2005.

Harvard Health Letter, "Reefer Rx: Marijuana as Medicine," September 2004.

Nadelmann, Ethan A. "An End to Marijuana Prohibition: The Drive to Legalize Picks Up," *National Review*, July 12, 2004.

Nicoll, Roger A. and Bradley N. Alger, "The Brain's Own Marijuana," *Scientific American*, November 22, 2003.

Nieves, Evelyn. "'I Really Consider Cannabis My Miracle': Patients Fighting to Keep Drug of Last Resort," *Washington Post*, January 1, 2004.

Saunders, Debra J. "Smoke Gets in Your Politics," *San Francisco Chronicle*, December 2005.

Schlosser, Eric. "Make Peace with Pot," *New York Times*, April 2, 2004.

Sharp, David. "Highs and Lows of Cannabis," *Lancet*, January 1, 2004.

Walters, John P. "No Surrender: The Drug War Saves Lives," *National Review*, September 2, 2004.

Web Sites

The Drug Enforcement Administration (DEA) (www.dea.gov/concern/marijuana.html). The DEA's Web site on marijuana focuses on the harmful risks and health effects associated with marijuana. It includes fact sheets, photos, trafficking trends, and more.

High Times (www.hightimes.com). The official Web site of *High Times*, www.hightimes.com celebrates the use of marijuana with editorials, event listings, and an activist center.

www.marijuana.com. This Web site claims to be the resource for all things related to marijuana, including marijuana policy reform and medicinal marijuana uses. It includes briefs on the latest marijuana legislation and court rulings.

Marijuana Anonymous (www.marijuana-anonymous.org). This Web site is the online presence of Marijuana Anonymous, a fellowship of men and women who seek to recover from marijuana addiction. A self-supported organization, Marijuana Anonymous offers twelve steps of recovery.

www.medicinalmarijuanaprocon.org. This Web site examines popular and effective arguments for and against the medicinal use of marijuana.

www.medmjscience.org. This Web site includes scientific studies, major reports and findings, and other opinions supporting the use of medicinal marijuana.

The Marijuana Policy Project (www.mpp.org). The official Web site of the Marijuana Policy Project, this site features up-to-date information about marijuana political campaigns and news. It also includes a library of marijuana reform publications and fact sheets.

National Institute of Drug Abuse (www.marijuana-info.org). This Web site includes research, general information, and fact sheets regarding the use and effects of marijuana.

Index

25
Drug Enforcement
   Administration (DEA), 45,
   46
   establishment of, 10
   on marijuana, 11
Drug Policy Alliance, 11
Deukmejian, George, 101

Emergency room admissions
   are increasing, 12, 15, 19–20,
     65, 86
   are overstated, 25–26
Epilepsy, 43

Fertility, 18

Gateway drug, 20
   marijuana described as, 11,
     56
Glaucoma, 42
Gonzales v. Raich (2005), 48
Government Accountability
   Office, U.S. (GAO), 92

Haines, Thomas H., 93
Hawaii, 68
Heart, 18

Incarceration, 11
Institute of Medicine (IOM),
   22–23, 27
   on effects of marijuana, 29
   on medical use of marijuana,
     42, 53–54, 61
Investigational New Drug
   (IND) compassionate access

program, 46

*Journal Canadian Medical
   Association*, 27
*Journal of the American Medical
   Association*, 56
*Journal of Trauma Injury,
   Infection, and Critical Care*,
   35–36
"Just Say No" campaign, 10

The Lancet (journal), 23
Laws, marijuana
   cost of enforcing, 11, 99
   origins of, 9–10, 45
Legalization
   argument against, 97–103
   argument for, 104–110
Lungs, 17–18

Marijuana
   Addiction, 56
     as exaggerated, 23–25
     youth in treatment for,
       64–65, 86
   affect on driving skills,
     28–33, 34–39, 57–59
   annual deaths from, 26
   arrests for, 25, 75, 82,101
   daily users of, 105
   drug classification of, 9
   harms of, are overstated,
     22–23
   health problems associated
     with, 11–12, 15–19
   incarceration for, 80–81
   media campaigns against,

Picture Credits

Cover: Photos.com

AP Images, 13, 19, 24, 32, 37, 40, 44, 51, 72, 94, 102, 108
AP Photo/Eugene Richards/VII, 76
© Henry Diltz/Corbis, 62
© Jeff Albertson/Corbis, 55
© Kim Kulish/Corbis, 69
Maury Aaseng, 16, 26, 30, 36, 47, 52, 64, 68, 75, 82, 87, 91, 100, 105